►Web 2.0 for Librarians and Information Professionals

Ellyssa Kroski

Neal-Schuman Publishers, Inc.

New York   London

Published by Neal-Schuman Publishers, Inc.
100 William St., Suite 2004
New York, NY 10038

Printed and bound in the United States of America.

The paper used in this publication meets the minimum requirements of American National Standard for Information Sciences — Permanence of Paper for Printed Library Materials, ANSI Z39.48-1992.

161-1296

Library of Congress Cataloging-in-Publication Data

Kroski, Ellyssa.
    Web 2.0 for librarians and information professionals / Ellyssa Kroski.
        p. cm.
    Includes bibliographical references and index.
    ISBN 978-1-55570-614-2 (alk. paper)
    1. Web 2.0. 2. Libraries and the Internet. I. Title.

Z674.75.W67K76 2008
020.285'4678—dc 22

                                                    2007043249

*To my husband Brian, my best friend
and my inspiration.*

CONTENTS

FIGURES AND TABLES

LIST OF FIGURES

LIST OF TABLES

FOREWORD

Welcome to *Web 2.0 for Librarians and Information Professionals*. I am pleased to be introducing this overview of some of the participatory technologies changing the way the Web works. What an incredible time the past few years have been during the advent of Web 2.0!

I first heard about Weblogs at the 2002 Computers in Libraries Conference. I started writing a blog called "Tame the Web" on April 1, 2003. The first post addressed my presentation at Computers in Libraries 2003. The mechanism of creating a post, publishing it, and seeing it live on the Web within seconds excited me. I read other librarian-authored blogs, and within a few weeks some of them had linked to my new blog. I was hooked!

At the same time, I started using other new tools. I adopted Rich Site Summary (RSS) feeds and the RSS aggregator Web site Bloglines (www.bloglines.com) to monitor library and information science news and blogs. I began to instant-message as a means to communicate with colleagues and friends. On May 10, 2004, I uploaded my first picture to the image-sharing community Web site Flickr (www.flickr.com). I was able to "tag" the photo of my Labrador retrievers Jake and Charlie, assigning my own keywords to describe it. These were all the trend-setting tools, and librarians were discussing them on their blogs. The time I have spent using the tools, learning about them, and talking about them with other librarians has been wonderful.

We should not, however, forget that librarians have used various mechanisms for social interaction and knowledge exchange over the years, from our publications, conferences, and symposia to the online forums and mailing lists such as PUBLIB in the 1990s. This history of physical and online interaction and conversation is long and varied in our field, as evidenced by publications such as Lerner's *The Story of Libraries*. With the advent of these new "2.0" technologies in the library world, the mechanisms for social interaction and the dissemination of information have changed yet stayed the same. Discourse that might have occurred at a conference is now played out via blog posts, comments, trackbacks, and other tools of the new Web.

In *Redesigning Library Services*, Michael Buckland argued that any new technology will have a significant effect on library services. Most striking for the discussion of social computing here is Buckland's contention that new delivery methods for information can change the way libraries work. "Consequently," he wrote in the Web version of his book, "a continuing quest for technological improvement has been and should continue to be important." This also can be applied to libraries and librarians: Learning and using new technologies can enhance and further our work and our mission as well.

So use Ellyssa Kroski's *Web 2.0 for Librarians and Information Professionals* for learning, exploration, and experience with the tools! Look for ways to meet your users where they are—with the tools they may be using. Enjoy!

Michael Stephens
Graduate School of Library and Information
    Science, Dominican University
Tame the Web: Libraries and Technology
    http://tametheweb.com

PREFACE

W
eb 2.0 technologies allow us to converse, communicate, and collaborate with library users as never before, and even reach non-users in new and exciting ways that might capture their attention. Blogs can offer readers timely and interesting library-related news. Wikis can hold information from library policies to specialized reference collections, and creating a library presence on social networking sites allows libraries to reach people in their comfort zone.

Web 2.0, most simply described as sites using participatory and collaborative technology, is growing at an astounding rate. Sites like MySpace, YouTube, and Wikipedia attract millions of visitors every day and are some of the most highly trafficked sites on the Internet. For those who are still becoming comfortable with the first iteration of the Web, understanding and using Web 2.0 technology can be intimidating. When I teach people about Web 2.0, they have three primary questions:

1. What is it?
2. Why is it important?
3. How can it work for me?

In *Web 2.0 for Librarians and Information Professionals*, I attempt to answer these questions by introducing readers to a vast array of cutting-edge tools. The first step to harnessing the potential of Web 2.0 is to understand the ways in which our users spend their time online, so each chapter covers the purpose, functionality, features, usage statistics, and software choices related to a major technology. Screenshots show the site or application in action, focusing on the most popular or representative example in each category. I also include an in-depth case study and several shorter real-life examples of how libraries and librarians are using the technology.

Many of these uses are surprisingly simple and can be undertaken even by those with limited technological expertise and for little or no monetary investment. Nearly all of the software applications discussed in this book are available for free or have some level of membership that is free of charge at the time of this writing. The featured ideas show how Web 2.0 can help libraries enhance their online presence, promote services, and increase patronage. Web 2.0 technologies also offer easy ways to connect with other libraries and librarians.

Anyone in the information field with an interest in Web 2.0 may find the information here useful. The potential benefits pertain to all library types, including academic, special, public, and school libraries. Effective use of Web 2.0 technologies allows libraries to be part of the global online community and truly collaborate with the people they serve. The one-way model of information provision can become a two-way conversation. *Web 2.0 for Librarians and Information Professionals* strives to provide inspiration for readers envisioning the practical uses of these technologies in their libraries.

ORGANIZATION

Each chapter in *Web 2.0 for Librarians and Informational Professionals* provides a self-contained module in which readers will discover information about a specific technology. The modules introduce the concept, discuss the ways in which librarians and libraries use it, and highlight some of the most prominent related sites. Even when one particular application dominates, the focus remains on the general concept, i.e., "Blogs" and "Social Bookmarking Tools," rather than the specific site, i.e., Blogger or del.icio.us. In this way, readers will gain an understanding of the technology's purpose and significance in order to make informed software choices. Screenshots point out the most important features of each site and help readers visualize its fundamental characteristics. The chapters are autonomous of one another, so readers may feel comfortable jumping to topics of interest.

The new Web offers equal access to a global conversation resonant with the voices of ordinary people. This constantly evolving participatory environment empowers people to contribute and create, as well as to consume. Today, people can share their stories, make friends, be heard, and express themselves creatively online. They can also work, collaborate, organize, store, and save. Technological innovations have transformed the Internet from a place to find and read information into a powerful way to achieve and grow. *Web 2.0 for Librarians and Information Professionals* seeks to facilitate this transformation within the realm of librarianship.

▶1
WEB 2.0

The World Wide Web is undergoing an exciting transformation that has come to be known as Web 2.0. It involves changes within Internet technology, as well as in the ways we think about and use the Web. We used to go online and were satisfied just to read static Web pages. Next, we progressed to limited participation with Internet sites through capabilities such as shopping transactions or posting to message boards. Now, the Web offers us a new and completely interactive experience in which we are invited to participate in creating and collaborating within a community. We are no longer relegated to the sidelines as passive bystanders on the Web, but have been empowered to be creators as well.

THE PARTICIPATORY WEB

Today's Web user thinks about the Internet in a completely new way. Web 2.0 has been aptly nicknamed the read/write Web because it enables people not only to read preset Web pages, but to write and contribute to them as well. And it is through our participation that we are able to author our own online experiences. Today we are writing reviews, commenting on news stories, uploading photos, organizing our favorite Web pages, and sharing digital video. What began with blogs and wikis has blossomed into an all-encompassing and standard phenomenon of sharing, collaboration, and user involvement. Web 2.0 marks the progression from static Web pages to dynamic, interactive ones, and the move from a one-way dialogue to the group conversation.

THE AMATEURIZATION OF THE WEB

Web 2.0 is a radical democratization of the Internet brought about by the development of software that lets ordinary users participate and express themselves on the Web. Today's Web applications have knocked down the technical barriers to entry so that even the least tech-savvy amongst us can become involved. Nowadays, photographers do not need to be programmers to display their portfolios on the

Web. Journalists and aspiring writers do not need to know HTML to have a blog—a Web-based journal. Ordinary people can upload their homemade videos alongside professionally crafted ones without any technical knowledge. By offering the average person Web-based applications with such a low learning curve, Web 2.0 evens up the playing field and creates an equilibrium that has never been possible before. The average person can put their work on the Web and have it judged by the community in a spirit of meritocracy. This new frontier gives people the opportunity to be discovered based on their talent and the value of their work. With Web 2.0, we have entered the age of the amateur.

THE SOCIAL WEB

Web 2.0 is a social phenomenon concerned with linking people to people, not just information. The new Web is about creating connections with other users, and it has brought about an explosion of growth in social networking and community-oriented Web sites. Through these online communities, people are not only creating and publishing content, but also sharing it with others. New social tools enable users to collaborate directly with others, or subtly unite to influence the will of the masses.

THE USER-FOCUSED WEB

The exciting evolution of Web 2.0 sees the user as the center of the virtual universe. Instead of expecting people to learn complex Web programming languages or forcing them to navigate unintuitive user interfaces, this second generation Web caters to user needs. Simple design, ease of use, and low learning curves are all top priorities for today's software developers. This new user-focused Web is inclusive by nature, taking into account the wants and desires of all users, not just those that make up the mainstream. This new sense of balance ushers in a golden age of the Web in which all users can participate, organize, read, write, and play online.

TENETS OF WEB 2.0

The term "Web 2.0" was originally conceived by the folks at O'Reilly Media in 2004 as a way to describe the post-crash Web, and at the same time to name an upcoming conference. Web 2.0 has come to mean a complete paradigm shift in the way that people create and consume information on the Web today. It is an evolution of Internet technology, which empowers users and puts them in control, enabling them to participate in and interact with the Web without technical knowledge.

From a software developer's perspective, the Web 2.0 mindset is about using the wisdom of crowds to develop better software, design simple and straightforward applications efficiently in response to user inclination, and share that technology so that others can build upon it. A set of basic principles or characteristics were identified by O'Reilly to represent the nature of the second-generation Internet. Those characteristics include:

The Web as a Platform

The Web is where everything is happening right now. It is the base, or programming platform, for which developers are designing new software. This new trend of Web-based software development brings with it the hope that all future applications will be available online in the form of a service or subscription, eliminating the traditional practice of installing numerous applications on one's own computer. Not only would this scenario simplify the user experience, it would make those programs portable and accessible from any online computer.

The Network Effect

This is the notion that a network, or a Web site community, is coincidentally improved as the number of people increases. Because Web 2.0 technologies are built around an "architecture of participation," people add value as they are participating in the community. For example, photographers who store and share their photos within Web 2.0 communities collectively amass a valuable store of user-created images. It stands to reason, then, that Web site communities that boast larger memberships are more valuable and enjoy a better network effect than smaller communities. Think of how unappealing it would be to join an online community which only had two other members!

Harnessing the Collective Intelligence

Sometimes referred to as the wisdom of crowds, this is the theory that when a Web site or network accumulates a large number of people participating within it, the collective, or group, becomes a filter for what is valuable. It stems from the belief that the many will always be more knowledgeable than the one. Amazon.com realized early on that by offering its users the ability to review books themselves, they would sort out the worthy resources from the inadequate. In Google's PageRank system, pages that have more authoritative Web sites linking to them hold more weight and rise to the top of search results pages. Web 2.0 companies hope to harness the collective intelligence of their communities of users in order to improve their systems.

Data Is the Next "Intel Inside"

While Web 2.0 companies create applications that allow users to participate by uploading photos, writing reviews, and creating content of other types, their motivation for doing so is not entirely selfless. The next generation of Web developers realize that it is this user-generated content that is the real value of their communities. Ebay is aware that users keep coming to their site, not to check out their great design, but to search their extensive database of user-created auction listings. Amazon.com knows that their unique value lies in their massive collection of user reviews. The goal of up-and-coming software companies is to design applications that are conducive to and will naturally generate this type of original content. Encouraging this participation is vital to Web 2.0 companies, because the more people contribute, the better the network effect and the collective intelligence.

End of the Software Release Cycle

Software traditionally has been released as a packaged product that users have to install on their computers. Patches and upgrades are periodically released as versions 1.1, 1.3, etc., pending a completely new version. On the Web, there is no need to install programs and patches. Software is delivered as a service. Upgrades and future versions happen seamlessly, most without the user's knowledge.

In the Web 2.0 environment, developers are much more attuned to the way the user interacts with the software. They use that knowledge to increase usability and add new features. Web 2.0 developers are able to "test market" features and get immediate feedback from their users. They consider the user a partner in the software development process. This characteristic of Web 2.0 is also referred to as the "perpetual beta" because the application is constantly being monitored and tested for usability and improved accordingly. There is never a "finished" version or product.

Less Is More

The philosophy behind developing for Web 2.0 is "less is more." Its objectives are simplicity and efficiency. Software startup companies are requiring minimal funding to design Web applications that do one thing, do it well, and are not top-heavy with ancillary features. This provides the user with a specialized application that has a very low learning curve. By designing light, adaptable applications, these companies are able to respond quickly to market needs.

Syndication

Sharing, not controlling, is paramount to the new Web. Authoring information in a structured format that can be used and reused is crucial for Web 2.0. A great example of this is RSS, or Really Simple Syndication, a technology that facilitates the syndication of content on the Web. A publisher (or blogger) publishes an article or posts to its site. An XML page is created (blogging software does this automatically), which users can access via an RSS link. That information can then be redistributed, reused, or reformatted by users, as well as read within a news reader. With Web 1.0, there was no standardized distribution method.

Design for Reusability

With Web 2.0 comes a philosophy of sharing, and this extends not just to users but to software developers, as well. Today's software developers are designing their applications to be shared in a standardized, structured way through an API (Application Programming Interface), a programming interface that enables other software to access the data and functionality of a Web site. Through these APIs, they can offer others the opportunity to use their technology in new and interesting ways. By using these APIs, tech-savvy users can combine two or more of these Web 2.0 applications to create a new one. This is referred to as a mashup. One of the best known mashups to date is Housingmaps.com. It is a combination of real estate listings from Craigslist.com with Google Maps, which allows house and apartment hunters to visually locate real estate listings on a local map.

Software for More than One Device

In today's world, users access information not only through their computers, but also through a slew of other devices, such as iPods, PDAs, cell phones, etc. Web 2.0 developers strive to create their software so that it is compatible with more than just the computer.

Rich User Experiences

Using Web 2.0 tools such as AJAX (Asynchronous JavaScript and XML), a new type of technology that allows information to be processed without reloading a Web page, developers can offer users a more compelling experience. With personalized start page applications such as Pageflakes and Netvibes, users can create modular home pages made up of moveable widgets, which are mini applications that drag and drop into place to display their RSS feeds, email, personal to-do lists, bookmarks, and more.

> **Widgets**, also called gadgets, are small applications that display structured digital content, often through an RSS feed. Widgets can display content ranging from blog feeds, Flickr photos, and Google documents to events calendars and to-do lists. Similarly, these gizmos are an effective way of displaying updates of sporting events, stock quotes, and news. These tools can be utilized both on the Web or on the desktop. They can display as well as aggregate content, and they can be dropped into aggregators themselves. These versatile applications can be found on the new breed of Web 2.0 start pages, portals, and community Web sites.

The Long Tail

The long tail consists of the less popular interests of users. It is called the long tail because, when creating a power law distribution chart to map out popular topics amongst users, the minority topics form a long tail leading to the end of the chart.

What makes the long tail interests so fascinating is that when they are added up, these non-mainstream interests far outnumber the popular ones. Between 25 percent and 40 percent of Amazon.com's sales come from the long tail, as do one-fifth of all Netflix rentals. The next-generation Web recognizes and embraces the long tail. Consequently, Web 2.0 applications are designed to serve not only popular but fringe interests as well.

Social Software

Largely, Web 2.0 is about community and collaboration through social software. These new applications help users streamline their daily lives, organize their data, and share it with others. Users can store and share photos through Flickr,

▶TABLE 1-1: New Web Characteristics		
New Web Characteristics	**Web 1.0**	**Web 2.0**
The Web as a Platform	Software releases designed for installation on individual computers.	Software is hosted online and is provided as a service.
The Network Effect	People browse Web content as a singular experience.	People participate in social communities, creating rich environments.
Harnessing the Collective Intelligence	The individual relies on personal knowledge.	The masses determine what is valuable.
Data Is the Next Intel Inside	Publishers create branded content.	Authentic content created by the user community is what has value.
End of the Software Release Cycle	Software, patches, and upgrades are installed by the user.	The perpetual beta, software as a service.
Less Is More	Feature-heavy software that takes training to use.	Simple, lightweight applications with a low learning curve.
Syndication	Web sites as individual silos of information.	Control relinquished in favor of distribution and sharing.
Design for Reusability	Software code is protected and kept private.	Application functionality and data is shared.
Software for More Than One Device	Software designed to run on the desktop.	Applications for Web, desktop, gadgets, mobile devices, iPods, etc.
Rich User Experiences	Web sites largely as text displays.	Web sites include AJAX, mapping, WYSIWYG editors, drag-and-drop functionality, etc.
The Long Tail	Only the most popular interests are catered to.	Everyone counts.
Social Software	Software as an individual experience.	Groups, collaboration, and mingling.

meet others on MySpace, and recommend news stories on social news aggregation Web sites such as Digg and reddit. For more tech-savvy users, Web 2.0 also includes sharing access to APIs, RSS feeds, and podcasting and video services. From the user's perspective, the Web is exciting again. It is about access to a dizzying array of new tools that have become available on the Internet, and most of them for free.

WHO'S USING WEB 2.0?

According to the Pew Internet and American Life Project, 75 percent of the U.S. population uses the Internet, and 96 million of these people have a high-speed broadband connection at home (Raine, 2007). Americans now spend an average of 14 hours per week on the Web, logging as much time online as watching television (Parr et al., 2006). The proliferation of high-speed Internet connections has made participation in the read/write Web an opportunity for everyone. Both teens and adults are using the new Web to participate in a number of activities:

Creating Online Content

▶ 51 percent of American teens have uploaded photos to the Web; 37 percent of all Internet users have done this.

▶ 39 percent of American teens share their original creations such as videos, stories, art, etc., on the Web; 22 percent of adults do the same.

▶ 28 percent of U.S. teens, 33 percent of college students, and 12 percent of adults have created a blog (Raine, 2007).

Consuming Online Content

▶ 85 percent of young Web users in the U.S. have watched online video.

▶ 46 percent of young Web users in the U.S. read blogs (Raine, 2007).

▶ 57 million adult Web users in the U.S. read blogs (Lenhart and Fox, 2006).

▶ 44 percent of young adult Web users and 36 percent of American adults use Wikipedia (Raine and Tancer, 2007).

Sharing Media

▶ 51 percent of young adults in the U.S. share photos online; 67 percent of older teens do the same.

▶ 22 percent of young adults in the U.S. share videos online; 17 percent of older teens do likewise (Raine, 2007).

Gaming

▶ 67 percent of American teenagers play online games with others (Raine, 2007).

► Membership in online gaming communities continues to grow in the U.S. and is projected to increase from the 3.7 million users in 2006 to 9 million by 2011 (Gartenberg and Horwitz, 2006).

Online Communities

► 55 percent of American teenagers have created a profile on a social networking Web site such as Facebook, while 20 percent of adults have created one of their own (Raine, 2007).

► 51 percent of MySpace users and 40% of Facebook's members are over 35 years old (Lipsman, 2006).

► MySpace has over 130 million users, Wikipedia over 5 million articles, and the blogosphere over 75 million blogs.

Both broadband adoption and content creation have been found to span class, education, and income levels. Web users earning less that $50,000 annually per household are actually somewhat more likely to put content online by a 46 percent–41 percent ratio, and the adoption of a high-speed connection at home among those with less than a high school education grew 70 percent between 2005 and 2006 (Horrigan, 2006).

WHY USE WEB 2.0?

The Web has become a giant ecosystem where people with diverse social, economic, and educational backgrounds can gather together to form communities of interest, create online content, and be heard. A place such as this, where the professional and the amateur co-exist and have the same sense of belonging and worth, holds enormous potential for libraries and librarians. Among the myriad of benefits of using Web 2.0 tools are the following:

Valuable Content Creation

Web 2.0 applications enable libraries and librarians to build powerful Web-based tools such as custom search engines, Web-based journals or blogs, knowledge repositories in the form of wikis, and shared media such as podcasts, videos, and photos, all without computer programming skills. These services provide amazing opportunities in the areas of library marketing, collaboration, communication, outreach, instruction, training, and resource development.

Patron Interaction

Web 2.0 tools allow libraries to enter into a genuine conversation with their users. Through new Web applications and functionality such as blogs, wikis, user comments, ratings, and reviews, libraries are able to seek out and receive patron feedback and respond directly. These social tools present the library from a personal perspective and offer the opportunity to form relationships with patrons.

Participation in Knowledge Communities

Libraries and librarians have the opportunity to take part in existing knowledge communities through the use of social Web 2.0 applications. Librarians can join and contribute to wiki endeavors, participate in answers communities and social news Web sites, and create a network of contacts to connect with in virtual communities such as Facebook, SecondLife, and MySpace. They may also choose to create their own social communities, such as the Library 2.0 social network.

Collaboration

Web 2.0 applications are particularly adept at facilitating collaboration between widely distributed groups of people. This can be quite useful in a library setting where staff members may be located on different floors or even in separate buildings. These tools can also assist libraries and librarians who wish to work in partnership with team members from distant libraries, or international colleagues.

TYPES OF TECHNOLOGY SOLUTIONS

Commercial software products, such as Microsoft Office, are pre-packaged solutions which are available at a fixed cost from a vendor. They provide a great deal of functionality right "out of the box" and are designed to get one up and running quickly. There usually are many instances of installations of the software, so case studies and best practices are readily available, and technical support is available from the vendor. One must bear in mind, however, that most of these systems are proprietary and consequently services are only available from the software vendor and its network of partners. This can make customization and integration with other systems difficult and costly, as it will likely require the vendor's expertise and professional services.

Much like commercial software, **open-source software solutions** can provide a wealth of functionality upon installation. Open-source solutions, such as MediaWiki and WordPress, differ from other packaged solutions because they are not created or controlled by a solitary vendor. They are usually maintained and developed by a community of individuals or companies in an open environment, which insures that no one individual can seize control of the software. This type of software, along with the underlying source code, is freely available for all to see, modify, support, or service. While those who choose to utilize these solutions may access the support of the robust open-source community, there is not anyone in particular who can be held accountable for software problems or technical support.

(cont'd.)

TYPES OF TECHNOLOGY SOLUTIONS *(Continued)*

Software services, also known as Web services, are programs that are licensed from application service providers, or "hosts." Unlike packaged software products, these are technology solutions in which the software and data reside at a remote facility and are managed by a vendor who is responsible for maintaining and insuring the proper operation of the systems and software. Many of these services, such as PBWiki and Flickr, offer a "free" solution option supported by advertising or other monetization strategy, while some require a subscription fee. These are potentially fast solutions for getting a system up and running quickly and usually at a lower initial cost than packaged software products. These solutions offer remote access, and most of today's new software services provide APIs that allow easier integration with existing systems. Prospective Web services subscribers will want to consider, however, that by choosing this type of solution they will be reliant upon a vendor for both the software application and the hosting services.

The **custom-developed solution** is one that your organization creates for your unique needs. This approach allows the most flexibility in both configuration and functionality. These solutions do not rely on software vendors for support or maintenance and can leverage the skills of your current technology team to build a solution that is tailored to your requirements and integrates with your existing systems. While solutions such as these offer clear benefits, they require the most effort to get up and running and can be quite costly in terms of time and resources. Custom-developed software solutions within the library realm include PennTags, the University of Pennsylvania Library's custom-made social bookmarking application, and MyOwnCafe, the social networking community created for the Southeastern Massachusetts Library System.

WEB 2.0 BEST PRACTICES

▶ **Create Technical Requirements.** Libraries will want to use these new technologies to solve existing problems or to make workflow processes run more efficiently, and not just for the sake of using "cool" new technology. You can be sure that you are on the right track by first creating a list of the requirements you need the software to meet in order to achieve the goals of your project. If you cannot create this list of needs, you may not "require" a software solution.

▶ **Check out What Others Are Doing.** It is always helpful to see how other organizations like your own are utilizing different technologies in order to meet their needs. This can provide you with an inspiration as well as a grasp of what some of the limitations might be of the various applications.

▶ **Ask the Community for Help.** You do not have to go it alone; there are plenty of people out there who are ready and willing to help you with your technical questions. Check out Yahoo!, Google, and Facebook groups, as well as specific technology forums and social networks, to ask for advice about new projects and to post about issues you may be experiencing.

▶ **Set Realistic Goals.** Set incremental and iterative goals for your team. These will seem more achievable by staff than the all-or-nothing approach. Offer incentives for people to realize targeted objectives.

▶ **Prototype.** Test the waters with free software to see if your concept works before investing serious time and resources. By starting small you can refine your initiative and then scale the project to your needs prior to making it public.

▶ **Consider Different Types of Solutions.** You will want to compare the pros and cons of different types of software solutions, such as those that you host yourself, those that are hosted by a service provider, free vs. fee-based applications, whether the software is open-source or proprietary, or alternatively if a custom-developed solution would better suit your needs. You will need to evaluate your organization's capabilities and consider questions such as whether you have the IT infrastructure to support hosting a project yourself, or if it would be better to outsource that function.

REFERENCES

Gartenberg, Michael, and Jay Horwitz. "U.S. Massively Multiplayer Games Forecast, 2006–2011." JupiterResearch (May 11, 2006). Available (for purchase): www.jupiterresearch.com/bin/item.pl/research:concept/111/id=97277

Horrigan, John B. "Home Broadband Adoption 2006." *Pew Internet & American Life Project* (May 28, 2006). Available: www.pewinternet.org/pdfs/PIP_Broadband_trends 2006.pdf (accessed December 12, 2006).

Lenhart, Amanda, and Susannah Fox. "Bloggers: A Portrait of the Internet's New Storytellers." *Pew Internet & American Life Project* (July 19, 2006), p. 14. Available: www.pewinternet.org/pdfs/PIP%20Bloggers%20Report%20July%2019%202006.pdf (accessed December 12, 2006).

Lipsman, Andrew. "More than Half of MySpace Visitors Are Now Age 35 or Older, as the Site's Demographic Composition Continues to Shift." *ComScore* (October 5, 2006). Available: www.comscore.com/press/release.asp?press=1019 (accessed December 10, 2006).

Parr, Barry, David Card, Zia Daniell Wigder, and Corina Matiesanu. "U.S. Entertainment and Media Consumer Survey, 2005." JupiterResearch (January 13, 2006). Available (for purchase): www.jupiterresearch.com/bin/item.pl/research:vision/63/id=96985

Raine, Lee. "Web 2.0 and What It Means to Libraries." *Pew Internet & American Life Project,* presentation given at Computers in Libraries 2007 Conference (April 16, 2007). Available: www.pewinternet.org/PPF/r/94/presentation_display.asp (accessed April 25, 2007).

Raine, Lee, and Bill Tancer. "Data Memo." *Pew Internet & American Life Project* (April 2007). Available: www.pewinternet.org/pdfs/PIP_Wikipedia07.pdf (accessed April 25, 2007).

▶2

BLOGS

With the advent of Web 2.0, we find ourselves in an age of participation—a time when all users are empowered to contribute, regardless of background or position. With the emergence of new Web 2.0 tools such as the blog, the non-technical person has been given a major voice online. Amateur writers are publishing their work alongside professional journalists, as the technical barriers to participation dissolve. Through the world of blogs, we are witnessing the democratization of the publishing industry.

A blog, or Weblog, is an online journal or Web site on which articles are posted and displayed in chronological order. Their content most often centers around a particular subject matter or theme. In essence, blogs have become the new "home page." A vast and widely distributed community of these Web-based journals has evolved, which has come to be known as the blogosphere.

Today, we are seeing Internet users blogging about everything from gadgets to their favorite "American Idol" contestant. They are blogging professional conferences live from their laptops, shedding light on scandals, and blogging their life stories. Professionals subscribe to industry blogs in order to keep current on the latest happenings in their field. One of the most valued characteristics of the blog is its currency, which cannot be rivaled by traditional media. Because they are not restricted by the constraints of the editorial process, bloggers have the ability to publish their material rapidly and in response to breaking news.

Blogging has become so prevalent that traditional publications such as the *Houston Chronicle*, *USA Today*, and *The New York Observer* have begun to offer editorial blogs for their readers' perusal. Organizations such as the ACRL (Association of College and Research Libraries) and corporations like Google and Microsoft have identified that blogging adds a human dimension to their otherwise impersonal institutions, and are blogging themselves. Networks of blogs such as LiveJournal and Gather.com have emerged as subset communities within the blogosphere. In these blog corrals, users congregate to blog about similar subject matter.

This rapidly growing phenomenon sees 120,000 new blogs created every day. The number of Weblogs surpassed 75 million as of April 2007 and reached a rate of over 1.5 million new blog posts daily, or 17 posts per second. This growth trend is indicative of the popularity of this new publishing medium, as the size of the blogosphere has doubled from 35 million to 75 million blogs in just under a year (Sifry, 2007).

Through the blogosphere, Internet users are participating in the read-write Web and providing valuable sources for news, opinion, and miscellany. This new style of journalism—unabashedly subjective and endearingly personal—represents a global conversation that is connected through its community of readers.

ANATOMY OF A BLOG

Blog templates and design vary greatly, but there are several features that are common amongst most blogs.

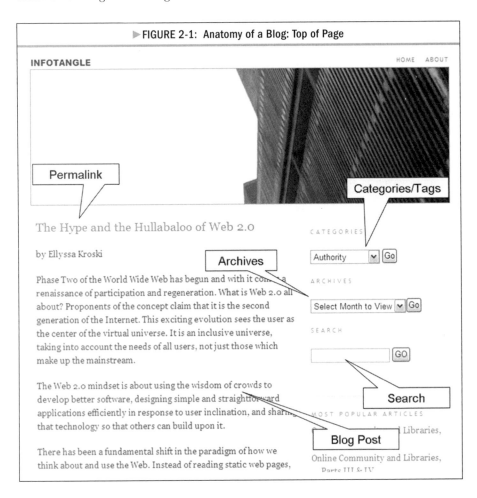

▶ FIGURE 2-1: Anatomy of a Blog: Top of Page

Blog Posts are the main ingredient in any blog. They are the written articles or entries in the blog. They are displayed down the center, or main portion, of a blog, one after another in chronological order. The most recent post will be at the top, with the rest following in receding order. Blog posts may contain images, illustrations, and embedded video, as well as text.

Permalinks are permanent links to particular blog posts. As new posts are added to a blog, older posts are pushed downward and eventually archived. For this reason, linking to the main blog URL is not an accurate way to link to an article that has been posted on a blog. The permalink pinpoints and provides an address for a particular post. On many blogs, the title of each blog entry is hyperlinked with the permalink. On others, the permalink can be found linked to at the foot of the post.

Categories, **Keywords**, and **Tags** can be assigned to each blog post as descriptors. In this way bloggers can develop their own taxonomy for their blog as an alternate form of navigation for their readers. By selecting a tag, users will obtain a results list of all posts that have been assigned that particular tag. Tags are often listed on a blog's sidebar, or can be contained in a drop-down box.

Archives are monthly or daily collections of blog posts. Most blogs display the posts for the current month only. All previous posts are automatically archived into corresponding monthly containers. Most blogs display a monthly calendar along the sidebar, which allows users to click on hyperlinked days in order to view the articles that were posted on that day. Users can browse to previous months by clicking on lists of months along the sidebar, or choosing from a drop-down box.

Search is a feature that is shared by every blog. Just as users can click on tags to browse posts, they also can search the contents of a blog by typing a keyword into a search box.

RSS Feeds are most often displayed along a blog's sidebar. These feeds allow the author to syndicate their content and readers to subscribe to the blog through their news reader. RSS feeds can appear as text links or as RSS symbols. (RSS will be discussed in more detail in Chapter Three.)

A **Blogroll** is a list of recommended links, which appears along the sidebar of a blog.

Author names are displayed at the beginning or the foot of blog posts. Many of today's blogs are collaborative, and there could be several different authors contributing articles. As each author signs in to create their post, their name is automatically attached to the entry.

Date and **Time** information is stamped on every blog post. On many blogs, the information about the exact date and time when the article was posted can be found at the foot of the post. On others, the date is displayed before a post or group of posts, and the time appears at the base of the entry.

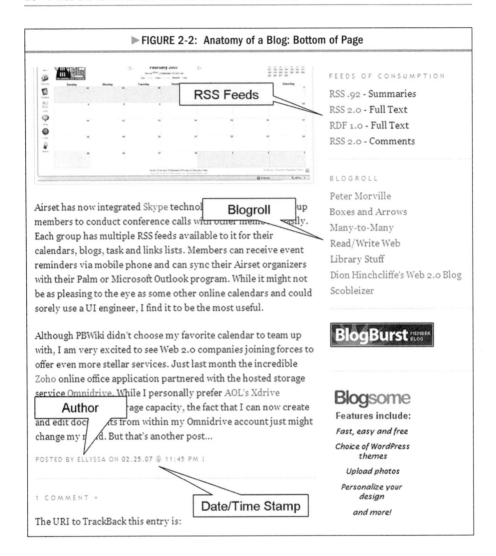

▶ FIGURE 2-2: Anatomy of a Blog: Bottom of Page

Comments epitomize the participatory spirit of Web 2.0, as they allow a two-way conversation between the author and the audience. At the bottom of every blog post is the list of comments made by its readers, and perhaps responses from the author. While some blogs have disabled this feature, most seize the opportunity to ignite discussion.

Trackbacks are virtual citations. They are notations that an author has cited and linked to a particular blog post on another blog or Web site. By following a trackback link, the author can find the article in which their post was mentioned. This interconnected feature that enables a two-way exchange is also representative of the new Web.

▶ FIGURE 2-3: Anatomy of a Blog: Comments View

3. **Le Web 2.0 existe-t-il ?**

   Comme tous les journalistes spécialisés, j'ai bien été obligé de m'intéresser au Web 2.0, ce concept inventé par Tim O'Reilly et qui fait actuellement fantasmer les foules (la première partie d'un dossier sur le Web 2.0 ...

   Trackback by Olivier De Doncker — January 15, 2006 @ 2:07 pm | Edit This

4. With Web2.0 the Web has entered a "golden" age of participation, the era of the amateur. A time of radical decentralization with innovations such as social software, the folksonomy, user tagging, the longtail. RSS, trackbacks, permalinks, comments,...

   Comment

   Comment by i-wisdom — January 15, 2006 @ 3:26 pm | Edit This

5. **Five Great Ways to Harness Collective Intelligence**

   Trackback

   Over the recent weekend I read Ellyssa Kroski's superbly researched and written new article, The Hype and Hullabaloo of Web 2.0. It's a must-read piece whether you're a die-hard aficionado or a battle-hardened detractor. The article is es

   Trackback by web2.wsj2.com — January 17, 2006 @ 5:40 am | Edit This

6. Thank you for this excellent summary.

   Comment by Mark Fuerst — January 17, 2006 @ 9:51 pm | Edit This

7. The article gives almost complete picture of Web2.0. I don't know whether the word "web 2.0", but I'm strong supporter of the ideas behind and I foresee the great change that's going to happen...power of sharing and colloboration..

HOW ARE LIBRARIES USING BLOGS?

Libraries have begun using blogs as a vehicle to promote their services, advertise events, and display book reviews. They are blogging about recent acquisitions, database upgrades, library renovations, and much more. Presented below are a case study and examples that demonstrate some of the more innovative uses of blogs in libraries.

Georgia State University Library Blog Collection
www.library.gsu.edu/news

The Georgia State University Library has a collection of 21 library news and subject-specific blogs, including a photoblog that displays library renovation images. Over

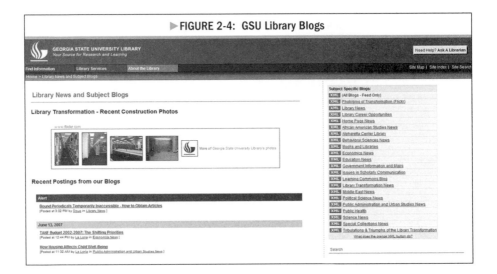

▶FIGURE 2-4: GSU Library Blogs

30 librarians contribute to these subject-related Web journals that provide patrons with up-to-date news and information for topics such as Economics, African American Studies, and Middle East News. The GSU blog collection was created in 2002 and began with just two blogs—one for library news and one for science bulletins.

Web Development Librarian Doug Goans saw a need for more dynamic Web pages for disseminating library news and events, while Science Liaison Librarian Teri Vogel wanted a means to communicate library resources directly to students and faculty. The two decided to team up and consolidate their technology initiatives. "Together we created a single blog system to support both our goals," said Goans.

After considering hosted solutions and third-party blogging software, the team decided to build a custom blogging application in-house. Support for multiple users was less robust at the time, and a custom installation would allow them to integrate the blog project into their existing Web efforts. Since they were already using a MySQL database for their Web site content, the team chose to use it to store their new blog data as well. The software was designed utilizing Active Server Pages (ASP), a Microsoft application development platform.

In an effort to publicize their new library blog collection, GSU library staff made announcements via e-mail and within their instructional workshops. As appropriate, the library's subject-specific research guides added links to the corresponding library blogs. The library blogs at GSU have proven to be a valuable communication tool and served to raise the profile of the Georgia State University Library within the community. Since their inception, the number of librarian bloggers has more than doubled, and the blogs have become an important source for news and events information for the library.

Although the technology choices were effective at the time, Goans has indicated that he would opt for an open-source solution that offers richer functionality and support if he had the choice today. "In fact, we are currently planning to upgrade from the in-house blogging application to an open-source product," he noted.

Mary Jo DeJoice, Head of Liaison Services, recently led the library in developing and implementing best practices for the blogs. Both DeJoice and Goans offer the following words of wisdom to potential library bloggers: set up policies and procedures at the outset for multi-user blogs; identify your potential audience and think about the role of your blog; put an assessment plan in place to measure your blog's success. (Doug Goans and Mary Jo DeJoice, e-mail correspondence with author, March 2007)

Other Ways Libraries Are Using Blogs

Library Web Sites

The Nebraska Library Association exchanged their conventional Web site for a blog-based library Web site at: www.nebraskalibraries.org, and the Lamson Library at Plymouth State University (NH) is beta testing its new blog home at: http://lamson.wpopac.com/library

Subject Resources

The librarians at Binghamton (NY) University have initiated a business blog on which they blog about electronic reference books, business database news, and statistical sources at: http://library.lib.binghamton.edu/mt/business, while the Mansfield Library at the University of Montana has created a resource for their state in which they post recently published government information and reports at: http://mt-govinfo.blogspot.com. The Virginia Commonwealth University Libraries pens a seasonal blog for Black History Month, which is active between the months of January and February each year at: http://blog.vcu.edu/blackhistory

Collaboration and Training

The Barnard College (NY) Library uses an internal staff blog to communicate with fellow reference staff members about departmental news, professional development, news from the field, and research tips at: http://barnardrefdesk.blogspot.com. The Learning 2.0 blog was conceived by the Public Library of Charlotte-Mecklenburg County (NC) to support a training program that involved hundreds of participating librarians at: http://plcmclearning.blogspot.com

Teens and Youth

The Lansing (IL) Library reaches its youth community on its Youth News Blog, with posts about ice cream socials and scholastic book sales at: http://lansinglibrary youth.blogspot.com. Similarly, the Darien (CT) Library has created a teens blog listing events such as pizza taste-offs, tech gadget talks, and knitting workshops at: www.darienlibrary.org/connections/teens

Class Materials

Mohawk College (ON, Canada) Library provides class notes and presentation slides supporting library workshops on their Class Notes blog at: http://mohawk lrc2.blogspot.com/classnotes

Book Reviews

The Waterloo (ON, Canada) Public Library reviews titles for its book club at: www.wplbookclub.blogspot.com

Library News

The Kelvin Smith Library at Case Western Reserve University (OH) blogs about library news such as database changes, university receptions, and digital video acquisitions at: http://blog.case.edu/orgs/ksl/news. The annual Long Island (NY) Library conference has created a blog to distribute conference news and information at: www.suffolk.lib.ny.us/lilc/

Library Leaders

The administrators of the Darien Library are blogging about the future of public libraries, community issues, and events on their Library Directors Blog at: www.darienlibrary.org/directorsblog, while the U.S. Library of Congress is blogging about libraries, curators, exhibitions, and history on their Weblog at: www.loc.gov/blog. Similarly, the team at the South Jersey Regional Library Cooperative have initiated a library consortium blog at http://sjrlc.typepad.com. The ACRL has joined the biblioblogosphere with this library association blog at: http://acrlblog.org, and the McMaster University (ON, Canada) Library's university librarian is blogging at: http://ulatmac.wordpress.com/

The **Biblioblogosphere** is a robust community of Weblogs written about issues relating to the library and information science fields. They are authored by a wide range of bloggers, including libraries and their patrons, library consortia, library associations, vendors and organizations, current and future librarians, and information professionals.

Discussion Groups

The Stafford branch of the Ocean County (NJ) Library posts links to reviews, news, and registration information for their DVD discussion group on their blog at: http://dvddiscussiongroup.blogspot.com. "Worthingteens" is a hip blog where teens can join book discussions, subscribe to RSS feeds, view a calendar of events, and take polls at: www.worthingtonlibraries.org/teen/blog

HOW ARE LIBRARIANS USING BLOGS?

From new LIS grads to ALA President Leslie Burger, librarians are using blogs to exchange and gather up-to-the-minute news and developments in the field. They are blogging conference sessions for their readers, sharing job experiences, providing summaries and statistics from industry reports, writing scholarly articles, and recommending resources. Librarians within the biblioblogosphere are in the middle of a dynamic and often scholarly conversation that has the reach of a broader audience and a more determined speed than traditional journals.

TechEssence.Info Collaborative Blog

http://techessence.info

Led by librarian Roy Tennant, a group of tech-savvy librarians merged their creative energies to create a collaborative library blog called TechEssence, which is targeted at library decision makers who seek straightforward explanations of information

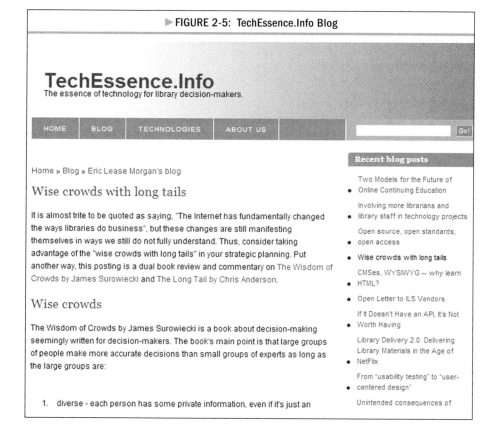

▶ FIGURE 2-5: TechEssence.Info Blog

technology solutions. These librarians share their unique experiences and personal expertise in the form of blog posts, as well as static pages summarizing key technology solutions.

BLOGGING SOFTWARE

There are two distinct types of blogging software: Those that are hosted online by a service provider, and those that the users must host and maintain themselves. While not all hosted blogging solutions are free, they enjoy the benefits of lower startup costs, low learning curves, and speedy setup. Conversely, in-house hosting awards it users with complete control over data and offers more flexibility in terms of integration.

WordPress
http://wordpress.org
WordPress is a free, open-source blog software created by startup Automattic Inc. It is available for download and install for those who wish to maintain their blog themselves, as well as a hosted solution for those who do not. WordPress has hundreds of features and plug-ins such as themes, tags, search, privacy options, and others. WordPress powers over one million Web-based journals, including the blogs of such well-known companies and organizations as Yahoo!, CNN, Harvard University, The New York Times, and The Wall Street Journal.

TypePad
www.typepad.com
Owned by SixApart, this hosted blogging solution ranges in price from $5 to $15 a month. TypePad offers its blog authors a WYSIWYG editor, categories, and community management features. Between SixApart's four blogging services— TypePad, Moveable Type, Vox, and LiveJournal—they lay claim to over 15 million bloggers (Holahan, 2006).

> **WYSIWYG** stands for "What You See Is What You Get" and is commonly utilized for HTML authoring. WYSIWYG editors enable Web site designers to create Web pages without any knowledge of HTML code, as they work within what is usually likened to an MS Word–like interface, seeing only a preview of what the document will look like upon completion rather than technical code.

Moveable Type
www.sixapart.com/movabletype
Although it offers free personal blogs, Moveable Type is a blog publishing platform geared toward commercial users. More businesses are utilizing this technology than any other blogging software. SixApart offers hosted and self-hosted

options for Moveable Type, as well as a wide array of features such as tags, widgets, customizable archiving, programming interfaces, and support for unlimited blogs.

LiveJournal
www.livejournal.com
This free hosted blogging community has 1.8 million active users. Bloggers can create private "journals" or blog within a social networking environment. Users can join communities and add friends in an atmosphere similar to MySpace. LiveJournal is based on open-source technology and is available to download for those ambitious users who wish to create their own communities.

Vox
www.vox.com
Vox is a private, free blogging network hosted by SixApart and aimed at users 25 and older. Users can determine privacy levels for each blog post, photo, video, or sound clip and can differentiate between friends and family.

Blogger
www.blogger.com
Owned by Google, Blogger is a free hosted blogging solution. Blogger allows its users to post photos, blog from their mobile phones, and post with a WYSIWYG editor. Weblog authors can create public or private blogs.

TOOLS FOR LOCATING LIS BLOGS

There are hundreds of library and librarian blogs on the Web today. Observing the many ways that others in the field have utilized this new technology can help spark creativity and determine best practices. The following resources provide access to the greater part of the biblioblogosphere.

LISWiki
http://liswiki.org/wiki/Blogs
Hundreds of library and librarian blogs are listed in this online library science encyclopedia.

LISZen
www.liszen.com
This is a search engine that indexes over 700 library and information science related blogs.

Blogging Libraries Wiki
http://tinyurl.com/pvzvp
Nearly 500 library blogs are cataloged by type in this comprehensive resource.

BEST PRACTICES

▶ **Keep Usability in Mind.** With all of the design templates out there for blogs, it is easy to get carried away with a slick-looking layout that does not offer the functionality that you need, or one that crowds in too many features and is confusing for the reader. When choosing a design for your blog, keep the end-user in mind; ask yourself if it is usable and intuitive.

▶ **Be Genuine.** Readers will be able to see through insincere marketing hype. If you are blogging for the right reasons, you will want to be open and informative about your organization and genuinely want to share news and opinion with your readers.

▶ **Keep Your Audience in Mind.** Do not try to be all things to all people—you will please no one this way. Decide who your audience is and then be a blog for teens, or for business students, or for patrons interested in library news, etc.

▶ **Stay on Point.** Keep your writing focused and consistent. Do not confuse your readers by posting about personal topics on a library or organizational blog.

▶ **Remember Your Brand.** If you are blogging for your library, you are the voice of that library online. This responsibility necessitates that you consider your library's viewpoint on topics as you post. Your library may have an established policy on blogging, and if they do not, you may want to develop one. For librarian bloggers, your writing is all that you have for readers to identify with; think about what type of image you want that writing to convey.

▶ **Encourage Participation.** If you are going to be blogging, you should enable comments from your readers. No one likes a one-way conversation, and readers will not hang around if they do not feel valued enough to be able to offer an opinion. Get over the fear that someone might say something negative about you or your library. If someone has something negative to say, they are surely saying it somewhere else; better to let them post it where you can address it directly. There is also the opportunity in these situations to gain valuable insight into how to improve library services.

▶ **Join the Conversation.** If your readers are leaving comments on a post you wrote, join in the conversation. Chat with your readers and let them know you are interested in what they have to say. This builds relationships with readers and keeps them coming back.

▶ **Make Sure Your Identity/Brand Is Visible.** If you are a librarian blogger, create an About page to let your readers know more about who you are and what you do. If you are a library or other organization, make sure your logo or name is somewhere on the front page of the blog, preferably at the top,

(Cont'd.)

REFERENCES

Holahan, Catherine. "SixApart's Booking Blogosphere." *Business Week* (September 24, 2006). Available: http://tinyurl.com/2cjkvo (accessed January 7, 2007).

Sifry, Dave. "The State of the Live Web, April 2007." *Technorati Weblog* (April 5, 2007). Available: http://technorati.com/weblog/2007/04/328.html (accessed April 20, 2007).

▶3

RSS AND NEWSREADERS

One of the most prominent progressions that marked the passage from the old Web to the new was the development of a standardized distribution method for online material. That method is RSS or Really Simple Syndication, a technology that enables publishers to syndicate news and other content on the Web. The simplicity of RSS has served to lower the barriers to the publishing process, allowing ordinary people to distribute their content to the masses. Amateur journalists, talk show hosts, and filmmakers have been enabled to distribute their content as easily as CNN.

The mechanics of RSS involve the publication of an article or post to a Web site. A related XML page is created, which people can access via an RSS link. That article, photo, or other content can be redistributed in any format the user prefers as long as it does not violate copyright. Most often it is disseminated through a user's news reader, such as Bloglines, NewsGator, or their Start page where it can be read either online or offline.

As with other Web 2.0 technology, RSS has evened the playing field and is allowing for the dissemination of information in ways that could never have been fathomed in the past. Today, a publisher of content describes everyone from *The New York Times* to bloggers, and includes the millions of people creating content on the Web. Because RSS has made Web content distribution an effortless task, there has been a meteoric rise in the amount of information available. Many of these new information sources not only provide outlets for alternative news, but publish their content for free, and through RSS deliver it directly to the user. Mainstream media has responded to this glut of information online by following suit with the release of their content. With the development of RSS, publishers have relinquished the stranglehold that they previously had over information and have given the user control of its management, utilization, and application.

Through this technology, publishers are sharing their own content while at the same time offering their readers highly focused information provided by other sources. National newspapers are presenting their news stories to readers alongside relevant blog posts made by approving independent bloggers, and local Web sites are providing their users with national news fed in through RSS feeds. RSS technology gathers bits and pieces of the Web and allows them to be reused in unique ways.

Today's Internet users are syndicating much more than blog feeds with RSS technology. They are creating mashups, personalizing content with widgets, and tapping into the pulse of the Web through connections, information, and other people. Armed with RSS, users approach the Web as an *à la carte* menu—no longer limited to one entrée; they selectively choose items that pique their interest. Instead of reading an entire newspaper, readers subscribe to appealing sections only. Rather than subscribe to a blog, users have the option to just read comments made on posts.

Internet users are tied into the best of the Web with RSS as it enables them to choose exactly what content to view. Through RSS, people can subscribe to tags, database searches, podcasts, video blogs, articles, blog posts, and even other users. RSS feeds allow users to aggregate personal and customized information into Start pages such as NetVibes and PageFlakes and portals such as MyYahoo! or a Google personalized page. These Web sites utilize the RSS standard to display news from readers' favorite blogs and journals, as well as a myriad of other sources such as their Netflix video rental queues, Gmail, and local weather. Through them, people are subscribing to their del.icio.us tags, feeding in photos from Flickr, and tracking their friends on MySpace.

A **Portal**, or Web portal, is a Web site that acts as a doorway to other pages or information available on the Internet that have been aggregated based on a particular subject or theme, and can sometimes be personalized. Personalized portals such as MyYahoo! enable users to create their own combination of information resources to be displayed on their portal page.

With RSS, people participate in the flow of information; like never before they are attuned to changes, shifts, and happenings. As blog posts are published, podcasts circulated, and weather updated, users are notified. When breaking news happens, users are made aware. Increasingly, control over online information rests with the new Web users who have been put in charge of their own consumption.

▶ FIGURE 3-1: RSS Symbols

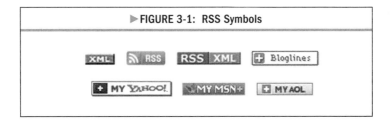

HOW ARE LIBRARIES USING RSS?

Libraries are utilizing RSS technology to share library news and content, as well as to gather and redistribute related information from other Web sources. Libraries are providing patrons with library news events updates, music and movie reviews, podcast, blog, and database search subscriptions, and promoting new acquisitions. Here is a look at how libraries are using RSS in new and interesting ways.

TCNJ's Course Management Library Feeds

The College of New Jersey (TCNJ) Library has integrated RSS feeds of new subject-specific books into their course management system. As the library acquires new titles, they are automatically fed into lists that are prominently displayed on course pages and subject guides. These feeds present students with relevant resources that can be found at the library through their class pages, and notify faculty when ordered library materials have been acquired. They also enable the library to offer dynamic subject guides to patrons, which automatically update.

This new library service was conceived by Systems Librarian Edward M. Corrado and Heather L. Moulaison, Cataloging & Modern Languages Librarian at TCNJ, who hoped to boost library visibility on campus. "We wanted to advertise the library and its print acquisitions in the online environment," Corrado reported.

▶ FIGURE 3-2: TCNJ Library RSS Feeds

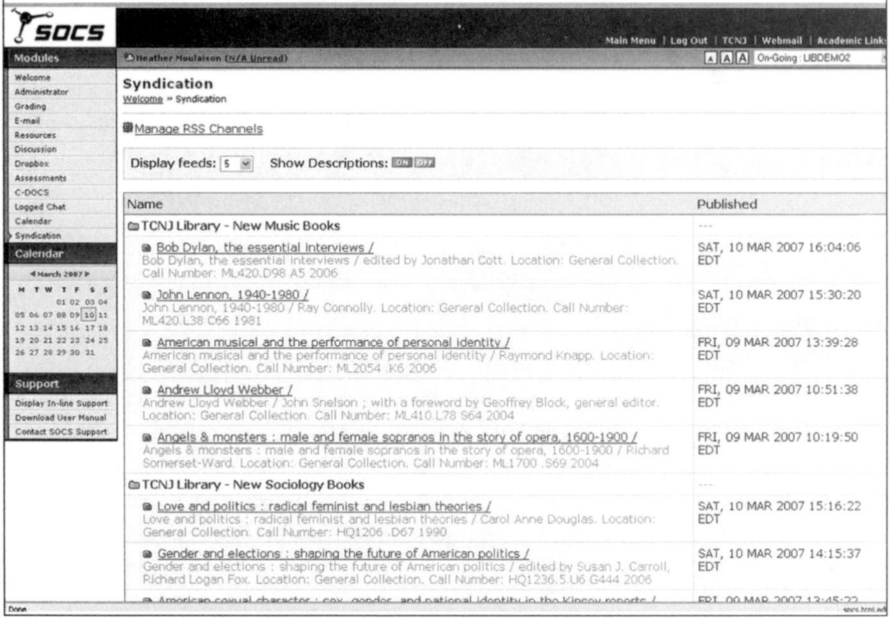

The TCNJ librarians teamed up with their IT department to create the RSS feeds using Structured Query Language (SQL), a programming language used to interact with a database, to draw the data from within their Voyager cataloging system. The programming language Perl was chosen to convert the files to RSS due to its rich-text processing features, as well as the organization's existing skill set with this technology. They utilized the scripting language JavaScript to display the RSS feed data within their Web pages.

The library publicized these new RSS feeds through announcements on their library home page, links within the library catalog, and through a campus newsletter story. They also found that word of mouth was a viable marketing tool and spoke to faculty at social events and during meetings. The IT staff felt invested in the project and also announced the news; "we cooperated with IT to create these feeds, so the IT people helped spread the word," said Moulaison. Next, the project team plans to present the news at an upcoming IT symposium for TCNJ faculty.

The faculty and library community at TCNJ has responded positively to the new feeds, both within the course management system and those within their subject guides. "Some of these feeds are among the most accessed resources on the library portion of TCNJ's Web site . . . the new DVD feed was the third most used resource in January 2007," commented Corrado.

Both Corrado and Moulaison are satisfied with the technology choices that were made during the project and would use them again. They would, however, focus more on marketing directly to faculty when introducing a new service such as this one. Based on their experience, they recommend that libraries not worry about having everything perfect at the outset of a project such as this one, but be willing to adapt and make changes after receiving feedback. According to Moulaison, "At first we only thought of putting the feeds into the course management system, but since we have adapted them to other uses and have had a better response." (Edward M. Corrado and Heather L. Moulaison, e-mail correspondence with author, February–March 2007)

Other Ways Libraries Are Using RSS

News and Events

The U.S. Library of Congress provides both general and specific RSS feeds for readers updating them about new Webcasts, news, and events, as well as digital preservation, Subject Headings, and current copyright legislation, at: http://www.loc.gov/rss/. Google news feeds are pulled into the home page of the Homer Township (IL) Public Library to provide local news to library patrons at: www.homerlibrary.org, and the La Grange Park (IL) Public Library allows patrons to subscribe to their events calendar with daily, weekly, or monthly RSS feeds at: http://tinyurl.com/39mvhq

Track Library Materials

The Hennepin County (MN) Library enables their customers to track due dates of their library items at: www.hclib.org/pub/search/RSS.cfm

Subject Guides

Georgia State University offers over 20 subject-specific RSS feeds from their blog collection to readers at: www.library.gsu.edu/news. The Kansas City Public Library offers RSS feeds for their numerous subject guides at: www.kclibrary.org/rss, while the New York Public Library offers their patrons a "Best of the Web" feed with links selected by NYPL librarians at: www.nypl.org/rss

Journal Articles

The University of Nevada, Reno Libraries supply a list of over 1,300 journal tables of contents feeds at: http://tinyurl.com/2vc3l7

Library Subscriptions

The Library Channel at Arizona State University offers listeners the chance to subscribe to library podcasts at: www.asu.edu/lib/librarychannel, while the Darien (CT) Library offers a page full of RSS feeds for users to subscribe to their many blogs at: www.darienlibrary.org/blogs.php. The South Carolina State Library redesigned their Web site with a content management system called Joomla, which offers their patrons RSS feeds for every single page at: www.statelibrary. sc.gov

Book Reviews

The Topeka and Shawnee County (KS) Public Library provides RSS feeds for book reviews, as well as reviews of movies and music, at: www.tscpl.org/rss.asp

New Acquisitions

The University of Nevada, Reno Libraries present users with RSS feeds that update users about new digital images that they have acquired at: www. library.unr.edu/ rssfaq.html, while the Templeman Library at the University of Kent (UK) offers its patrons a new acquisitions feed at: http://library.kent.ac.uk/library/newbooks/ rss.shtml. The New York Public Library provides an RSS feed for new database subscriptions at: www.nypl.org/rss, and the Tacoma (WA) Public Library offers RSS feeds for new DVDs by genre at: http://tinyurl.com/2wmsvp

Library Workshops

The University of Alberta (Canada) uses RSS feeds to keep patrons updated about new library instruction and training workshops at: www.library.ualberta.ca/student training

Catalog Searches

Patrons can save their catalog searches in the form of an RSS feed at the Hennepin County (MN) Library at: www.hclib.org/pub/search/RSS.cfm

HOW ARE LIBRARIANS USING RSS?

Librarians are keeping up to date by subscribing to news and information sources such as blogs and library journals via RSS feeds. They are saving database searches for future research and subscribing to them through news readers. Finally, they are publishing content on their own blogs and Web sites and syndicating it for others to read and use.

PubMed Searches

www.pubmed.com

It is now possible to save searches made in the PubMed database as RSS feeds. Librarians and students alike have the ability to take advantage of this useful feature of the medical database. PubMed creates these custom feeds on the fly for users who select to send their searches to an RSS feed.

▶ **FIGURE 3-3: Saving Searches as RSS Feeds**

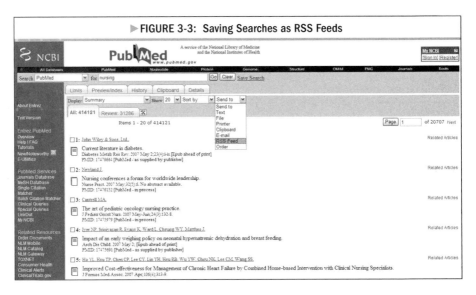

NEWS READERS

Everyone has a collection of Web sites, online publications, and even people through which they get their news. By subscribing to these sites, blogs, people, tags, etc., via an RSS feed in a news reader, people can view the newest items from that source, as well as those that have been recently changed. This saves people the time and trouble of returning to each Web site to monitor what has been added or altered. News readers allow users the ability to read RSS feeds by transforming XML files into a human-readable format. Once users have subscribed to their RSS feeds, the news aggregator continues to display updated headlines, synopses, comments, or full postings from each Web source. News reader software is available in three main types: Web-based, desktop applications, and browser-based.

Online News Readers

These Web-based applications are available from any computer with an Internet connection, which makes reading subscriptions portable. Many of these have incorporated social features into their programs, such as feed sharing and tagging, as well as user-ratings and friends. Hybrid online news readers include start pages (discussed in Chapter 9) and portals such as MyYahoo! and MyMSN, which offer RSS feed reading capabilities, although it is not their primary purpose.

Desktop News Readers

Desktop applications that are available for download offer users the benefit of synchronization, which is the ability to download feeds for future consumption. Although news reading is limited to one computer with this application type, these applications tend to operate faster than online readers and offer more powerful capabilities, such as listening to music or watching videos straight from the RSS feed.

Browser-Based News Readers

RSS feeds can now be subscribed to directly through the browser interface. Subscribing to Web pages is an option available through the bookmarks or tools menu on many of today's Web browsers including Firefox, Microsoft Internet Explorer (version 7 and up), and Safari. RSS feeds are listed within the bookmarks folder and display the latest headlines as subfolders or within the browser itself. This is a fast and easy way to subscribe to Internet Web sites while browsing, but it is not portable, as the subscriptions reside within the browser only.

NEWS READER FEATURES

Although there are many different types of RSS readers available today, there are some features that are shared by the majority of them.

The **Feed List** is the listing of RSS feeds to which the user is currently subscribed. As feeds are added to the list, users are given the option to designate a folder in which to place them. Each feed displays the name of the news source and the number of new items. Clicking on a feed in the feed list will result in the display of the latest items in the reading pane.

Search is the means by which many RSS feeds are found by users. When users perform keyword searches of available Web feeds, they are given the option to

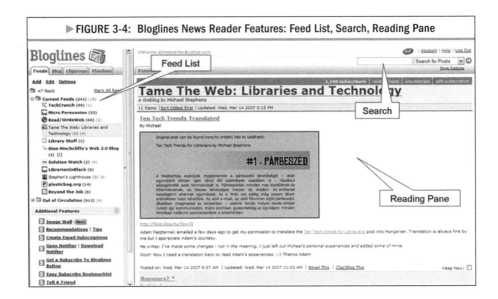

▶FIGURE 3-4: Bloglines News Reader Features: Feed List, Search, Reading Pane

subscribe to them from the results list. Some news readers offer users a preview before committing to acceptance of the RSS feed.

The **Reading Pane** is the main area where the headlines and summaries of news items are displayed. In it, users can read and interact with news posts and headlines.

A **Clippings folder** is a feature offered by nearly all readers. It is a folder to store headlines and story items for future retrieval. As people read items in the main reading pane, they are offered an option to clip individual items. Clipped stories and posts may be organized into a main folder or into user-created subfolders.

The **Add Feed** option allows users to manually add an RSS feed by copying and pasting its URL into the provided form.

Mark as Read is similar to the e-mail function of the same name. With this feature, people can globally denote that all items belonging to individual feeds have been read. This will eliminate the parenthesized numbers alongside the feeds.

Date Sort enables people to arrange items according to their age. Many aggregators allow this functionality, which toggles between displaying items that are newest and items that are oldest.

Mark New is a feature that, unlike its counterpart *Mark Read* allows people to designate all items within a feed as new or unseen. Many programs also offer the option to mark individual items within a feed as unread.

E-mailing an article, blog post, or other item from a news aggregator is a common function which is offered by nearly all programs.

The **Clip** action is a way to save items within a clippings folder, or to subfolders to read at a later time.

▶ FIGURE 3-5: Bloglines News Reader Features: Add Feed, Mark Read

▶ FIGURE 3-6: Bloglines News Reader Features: Date Sort, E-mail, Mark New, Clip

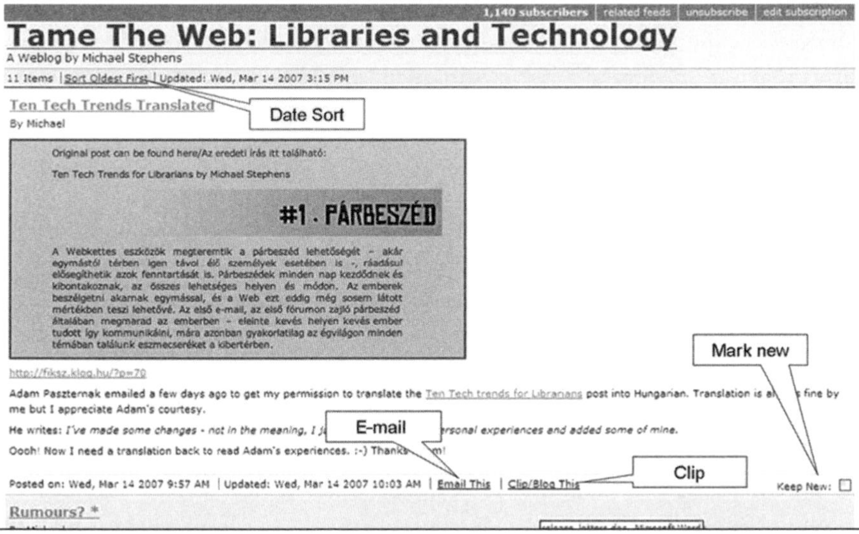

NEWS READER SOFTWARE

Bloglines

www.bloglines.com

A property of Ask.com's IAC Search & Media, Bloglines indexes tens of millions of live content feeds and is available in ten languages. In addition to the core set of features, this Web-based reader offers social functionality, such as blogroll sharing and user blogs, a mobile version for handhelds and cell phones, and a blog search.

Google Reader

www.google.com/reader

The Google online news reader offers its users the capability to share items with friends through a public Web site and subscribe to news sites as they browse the Web through a Google Reader bookmarklet. The Google Reader is available in mobile format and as a Google Gadget, which can be added to the Google personalized start page.

> A **bookmarklet** consists of a button, which resides on the Web browser, that can be clicked to create a Web site bookmark that is stored online within applications like Google Reader or del.icio.us. The bookmarklet is a mini application that submits the page information, including the link URL of the Web page the visitor is browsing at the time of the click, to its parent application.

Rojo

www.rojo.com

This online reader's unique name means "RSS with mojo." Rojo has implemented several social features within its reader, such as member voting and tagging of stories, contact lists, and the ability to sort stories by relevance rather than date in order to view the most popular items within subscribed feeds first. Rojo presents stories that other members are reading, as well as the most read, tagged, and mojo'd stories within a host of categories.

NewsGator

www.newsgator.com

This slick RSS news reader offers a free online version, as well as a suite of options for the desktop, which are available for purchase. NewsGator users can rate stories as well as e-mail and IM them to friends. Videos and podcasts can be browsed from within the reader or downloaded with a click to the free FeedStation podcatcher provided by NewsGator.

Live Bookmarks

www.mozilla.com

Live Bookmarking is a method of subscribing to RSS feeds via a Web browser. The option to "Subscribe to this page" is available within the Bookmarks folder, or a bookmarklet button; however, the browser will also query the user when on an RSS feed page. The latest stories from subscribed RSS feeds are displayed in the bookmarks folder or in the browser sidebar for easy access.

RSS TOOLS

Create RSS Feeds

There are many applications available that will allow people to create and edit RSS feeds for their Web sites. Some of these programs include:

Feedburner: www.feedburner.com
FeedYes: www.feedyes.com
FeedForAll: www.feedforall.com (fees may apply)
Feed Editor: www.extralabs.net (fees may apply)
RSS Creator: www.Webreference.com/cgi-bin/perl/makerss.pl

Note: These are tools to create RSS feeds manually, and all subsequent updates to the Web site will also need to be added manually to the feed. In order to create an automatically updating RSS feed, it is necessary to do some programming or work within a content management system that has this functionality available, such as a blog.

Republish Content via RSS Feeds

Interested in pulling in headlines from the *New York Times Book Review* onto your Web site, or local information via Google News? Free Web tools are available that will create Javascript code for you to cut and paste onto your Web site in order to display news feeds. Among these tools are:

Feed2JS: http://incsub.org/feed2js/
Feedroll: www.feedroll.com
FeedSweep: www.howdev.com/products/feedsweep
Feedsplitter: http://chxo.com/software/feedsplitter

Remix RSS Feeds

RSS Mixers are new tools that allow users to create new RSS feeds from several existing feeds. These remixers are fantastic tools that can be used to create custom RSS feeds for specific subject areas. Some of these tools can be found at:

FeedBlendr: www.feedblendr.com
Frankenfeed: http://frankenfeed.com
RSS Mix: www.rssmix.com
FeedJumbler: http://feedjumbler.com

RSS to E-mail

If you or your staff do not want to subscribe to a news reader in order to browse RSS feeds, but still want to keep up, RSS-to-e-mail tools may be for you. These tools allow users to subscribe to RSS feeds that deliver news and updates directly to their e-mail inbox. These tools are available at:

Squeet: http://squeet.com
R|Mail: www.r-mail.org
FeedBlitz: www.feedblitz.com
Feedburner: www.feedburner.com/fb/a/publishers/fbemail

BEST PRACTICES

RSS

▶ **Offer a Variety of Subscription Options**. Some people will want to read the summaries of your news items/blog posts in their news readers, while others will want to read the entire article, and still others will opt only to read the comments, or will be looking for an e-mail feed. By offering multiple feed options, you will maximize your number of subscribers.

▶ **Make Feeds Visible**. Do not make readers search your site in order to subscribe; most will not go through the effort. Use standard orange RSS or XML buttons to indicate subscription options.

▶ **Create an FAQ Section**. Many people still do not know what RSS is, and those who do are not necessarily confident about how to subscribe. Create a "Frequently Asked Questions" or "What is This?" page to which you can link directly under the RSS image, and feed options that will explain what RSS is, the subscription options you are offering, and exactly how to subscribe to the feed in a news reader and/or portal page such as MyYahoo!

▶ **Offer Useful Content**. Think about the type of information you would want to be kept updated on, such as new blog posts, library events and happenings, library news, new database subscriptions, new workshops and classes, new acquisitions, books you have placed on hold, your library book due dates, changes to subject guides, etc.

▶ **Choose Third-Party Content Wisely**. When pulling in content from external news sources via RSS, think about whether that information will be on-topic and relevant for your readers. Just because you *can* use RSS feeds to easily draw in third-party content does not necessarily mean you *should* be doing so for your library. A music library, for example, will probably not benefit by pumping in headlines from the *Wall Street Journal* on the front page of their Web site. Additionally, make certain you are respecting copyright laws when utilizing third-party RSS feeds.

▶ **Consider Work-Arounds**. If you do not have the technical know-how or the staff on hand to create your own RSS feeds, consider some technology solutions that offer them automatically, such as blogs, wikis, Web 2.0 applications, etc. Be creative and think outside the box for some of your RSS needs. Use free online event communities such as Eventful.com or Upcoming.org, which offer RSS feeds, to list your library's events or workshops calendar, post your news and happenings on a blog which can be subscribed to, and post your photos of library events on Flickr, which lets interested viewers subscribe via RSS feeds.

(Cont'd.)

BEST PRACTICES *(Continued)*

▶ **Market Your Feeds**. Let your patrons know about the exciting content they can subscribe to via your new RSS feeds by posting about it on your blog, linking to it on your library Web page, sharing the news with library bloggers and others in your community.

News Readers

▶ **Organize News Feeds**. Avoid information overload by organizing a large amount of feeds into "Everyday" and "Occasional" folders, representing feeds that you read daily to stay updated and those you read at a more leisurely pace. This reduces the amount of information you need to deal with on a daily basis while still keeping you subscribed to the feeds you feel are important.

▶ **Utilize the Clippings Folder**. When you come across useful items that you think you will use as resources for current or future projects, add them to your clippings folder for later retrieval. It is extremely helpful to organize your clippings folder into subfolders for each of your research areas, so that you can add new resources directly into those specific folders.

▶ **Use Mark New**. If you come across a post that you want to investigate further but just do not have the time that day, you can mark it as new so that it will keep appearing in your reader every time you access that feed. This is very useful as a personal reminder to read an article or follow a link. You can also use the Mark All New to keep all the news items in that feed until you have a chance to read them. This comes in handy when you are interrupted or have to sign off unexpectedly.

▶ **Start Fresh**. If you leave on vacation or fall behind in reading your feeds, they can really pile up and become overwhelming. Instead of avoiding your news reader, start fresh when you return. Do not worry about missing a crucial piece of news; if it is important, it will come up more than once and probably in more than one of your feeds.

►4

The arrival of the read/write Web ushers in a spirit of cooperation and community, an atmosphere in which all users have been sanctioned to contribute expertise to their own online resources. Wiki technology provides an arena for effortless collaboration and knowledge sharing among a community of users without any programming knowledge. It allows team members to brainstorm, gather subject expertise, work together on projects, create training resources, and replace intranets. This new form of bottom-up, social publishing harnesses the wisdom of crowds and defies barriers such as time, place, and technical know-how.

From the Hawaiian meaning quick or fast, a wiki is a collaborative online space in which many users can work together on a shared project. A wiki allows community members to participate in the creation of Web sites and documents quickly and easily, and without HTML knowledge. This new collaboration tool enables a distributed set of users to edit and overwrite existing content, create new content, or revert back to previous versions. Grassroots by nature, wiki efforts develop organically as users generate content and contribute to the organizational structure of the wiki.

The largest and most recognizable wiki to date is Wikipedia. Open to the public for both editing and consumption, it enjoys a community of over 100,000 worldwide contributors who have supplied its 5 million articles that have been written in over 200 languages. The most massive encyclopedia in the world, Wikipedia offers useful information on topics ranging from country profiles, to card game rules, to sports figure biographies.

Ordinary people are contributing to public knowledge repositories by offering destination information to the WikiTravel community, supplying legislative information within the Congresspedia, and building the world's largest how-to manual through wikiHow. Networks of wikis have developed, such as the Wikia collective with over 2,000 individual wiki communities, including, among others, the political "Campaigns Wikia" and the *Star Wars* fandom wiki, the "Wookieepedia," which has over 40,000 articles.

Increasingly, wikis are being put to use within corporate settings. Within these private wiki environments, businesses can tap into the collective intelligence of their own pool of resources. The Intellipedia, a project of the Director of National Intelligence (DNI), along with the CIA Wiki, are both internal and classified wikis. Production company Ascendant Films used a private wiki to manage all of the financing and production paperwork for the film *Lucky Number Slevin.* Corporations such as Bank of America, Glaxo Smith Kline, and the BBC are but a few of the thousands of organizations that have adopted wikis as collaborative staff-side tools. Indeed, the Gartner Group has predicted that "half of all companies" will use internal wikis by 2009 (Levine, 2006).

Leading software developers have seen the writing on the wall and rolled out wiki functionality within their enterprise solutions, such as Microsoft's SharePoint and Intel's Suite Two. Google has acquired the enterprise wiki JotSpot. These speedy software programs were granted legitimacy in March, 2007, when the word "wiki" was added to the Oxford English Dictionary Online along with 287 other new words.

WIKI FEATURES

Wikis can vary greatly in both their appearance and purpose. Open to the public or limited to a private community, for purposes of outreach or use within the enterprise, wikis are invaluable devices for collecting dispersed knowledge. Although

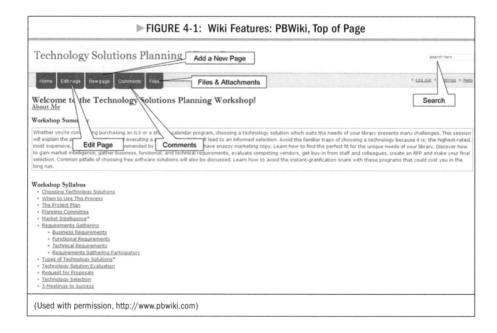

▶ FIGURE 4-1: Wiki Features: PBWiki, Top of Page

(Used with permission, http://www.pbwiki.com)

wikis are being cultivated in a host of different ways by Web users, they do share a set of features common to almost all wikis.

To **Add a New Page** to most wikis, users simply need to click on a button or link. Many wiki applications provide users with a WYSIWYG interface similar to popular word processing systems. Users can type their content into the space provided and utilize toolbars for formatting text and adding links. Wikis also utilize a specific wiki syntax that is easier to learn than HTML and can be employed to further customization.

Edit Page functionality is a standard feature of wikis, as well as a powerful collaboration tool. On a wiki, any user with access to a page can take part in creating and editing it. Users can make changes to previous versions, delete them, overwrite them, or revert back to an earlier state.

Search functionality facilitates the user's ability to find relevant information within these collaborative and sometimes massive online spaces. Users may not only browse wikis by an index of pages, but can conduct keyword searches to locate relevant data.

Comments can be made on any page within a wiki. Members of the wiki community can use this social feature to discuss the development of the wiki or topics of particular pages.

Files and Attachments can be uploaded to wikis. Users can add images to wiki pages, as well as documents, spreadsheets, and other files. This feature is particularly useful for communities that are utilizing wiki technology as a knowledge-base, online manual, or intranet.

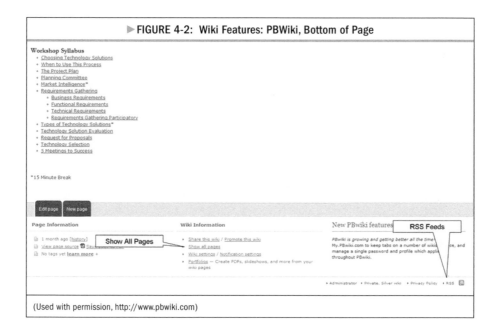

▶ FIGURE 4-2: Wiki Features: PBWiki, Bottom of Page

(Used with permission, http://www.pbwiki.com)

▶ FIGURE 4-3: Wiki Features: PBWiki, Revision Comparison

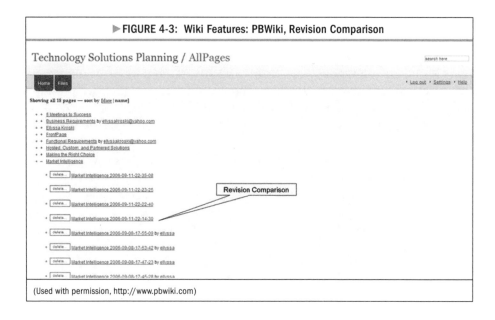

(Used with permission, http://www.pbwiki.com)

▶ FIGURE 4-4: Wiki Features: PBWiki, WYSIWYG Editor

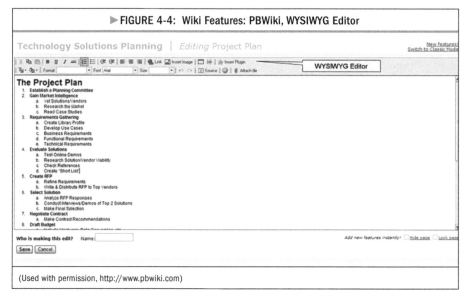

(Used with permission, http://www.pbwiki.com)

Show All Pages provides a directory of every page that exists within a wiki.

RSS Feeds are available for notification of changes made to the entire wiki, or only those made to a particular page. Rather than manually checking for edits or new page additions to a wiki, community members can subscribe to the provided RSS feeds to receive automatic updates whenever a change is made.

Revision Comparison, sometimes also referred to as "History," provides a detailed listing of all edits, additions, and changes that were made on a particular page of a wiki. Most wiki programs allow users to compare versions in a side-by-side view. This history facilitates reverting back to a previous version—a vital tool in a collaborative environment such as a wiki. Access to such historical versions serves as a safety net in case of mistakes, inadvertent deletion of text, or graffiti.

WYSIWYG Editors may be found within most wiki applications. They provide an easy-to-use interface for wiki creators to produce content. Similar to the Microsoft Word interface, a WYSIWYG editor provides formatting toolbars along with a window in which documents, links, and other material can be created without any HTML code.

HOW ARE LIBRARIES USING WIKIS?

Libraries are using wikis to provide patrons with subject-focused resource collections, to offer community tools for participation and collaboration, and to create knowledge bases. They have begun to utilize this new technology to gather the tacit knowledge of library staff, to brainstorm in teams, and to cooperate on local and global projects.

Wyoming Authors Wiki
http://wiki.wyomingauthors.org
The Wyoming Authors Wiki is an online biographical resource filled with over 800 pages of information about authors native to "The Cowboy State," as well

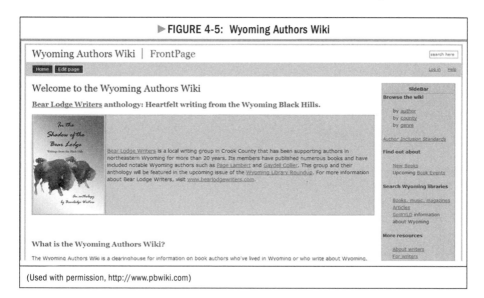

▶ FIGURE 4-5: Wyoming Authors Wiki

(Used with permission, http://www.pbwiki.com)

as those who have written about it. A project of the Wyoming Center for the Book and helmed by Coordinator Susan Vittitow and intern Jill Armetta, the wiki launched in the summer of 2006 as an online space where contributors could supply biographical research about authors, the books they have written, and upcoming speaking engagements. The wiki may be browsed by author, county, or genre and can be limited to living authors or those who write about the state.

The Wyoming Authors Wiki was planned as an alternative to an existing database that demanded considerable staff resources and had become a challenge to keep updated. "The Wyoming State Library saw an opportunity to improve the quality and timeliness of the content while reducing staff time," said Vittitow.

Vittitow and her team sought a hosted software solution for their wiki due to the quick-start timeframe and the ease of customization. "We decided it was more effective in terms of staff time to use a hosted wiki, focus on the content, and let someone else deal with the tech side," she commented. After testing several wiki farms, they resolved to go with the PBWiki program because of their access controls, custom domains, and easy editing interface.

The organization printed up hundreds of Wyoming Authors Wiki bookmarks to market the project and distributed them at events such as the National Book Festival, and at outlets such as bookstores and libraries. They issued a press release and published an article in their "Wyoming Library Roundup" that was distributed to several thousand in their community.

In only six months, the wiki has attracted over 50 contributors who are adding their own knowledge to the collection by editing and creating new pages. "We've gotten much more information than we could have entered with limited staff time," remarked Vittitow. "We've had authors contribute who have done biographies of other Wyoming authors, so we've gotten the benefit of their research."

The Wyoming Authors Wiki has not only garnered attention within their local community, but reached an international audience as well. Vittitow has fielded inquiries about it from librarians as far away as Australia and Denmark.

Although Vittitow wishes that PBWiki had an easier registration process while still allowing for access control, she would use the software again and would recommend it for libraries. She advises other libraries who are undertaking a wiki project such as this one to be sure to seed the wiki with information at the outset. "No one contributes to a blank wiki—it's too intimidating," Vittitow said. She also counsels libraries to do all they can to market their projects and be patient, as it often takes time to build up a user community. (Susan Vittitow and Jill Armetta, e-mail correspondence with author, February–March 2007)

Other Ways Libraries Are Using Wikis

Subject Guides

The St. Joseph County (IN) Public Library has created a wiki subject guides portal at: http://tinyurl.com/yr8lns, while the Ohio University's Biz Wiki provides researchers with focused business information resources at: www.library.ohiou.edu/subjects/bizwiki

Library Resource Reviews

The Butler University (IN) Libraries allows its students, faculty, and staff to review its reference resources on its ButlerWikiRef at: http://tinyurl.com/yvxlvo

Intranets

The University of Connecticut Libraries' Staff Wiki contains over 900 pages related to its Information Technology Services, including service call logs, staff manuals, and knowledge bases, at: http://wiki.lib.uconn.edu/wiki, while the University of Minnesota Libraries utilizes a wiki as a staff Web site that includes human resources, payroll and communications information, as well as policies, procedures and staff charters at: http://wiki.lib.umn.edu

Staff Training

The library staff at the Antioch University New England (NH) Library have created a Staff Training and Support Wiki for the library's front desk, which includes everything from circulation policies and notices to instructions for opening the library at: http://tinyurl.com/28672j

Library Web Sites

Wikis are powerful content management systems that can be tailored to serve as a library's Web site, as evidenced by the USC Aiken Gregg-Graniteville (SC) Library's Web site at: http://library.usca.edu

Event Planning

The ALA supports its annual events and midwinter meetings with conference planning wikis that provide community information and guides to the local environs, as does this one at: http://wikis.ala.org/midwinter2007/index.php/Main_Page

Collaboration and Learning

The Mesquite (TX) ISD Library Advisory Committee is using a wiki to collaborate on its mission statement document at: http://libadvisorywiki.pbwiki.com and the New Tech Wiki created by the State University of New York Library Association

(SUNYLA) tracks how libraries in the SUNY system are utilizing new and emerging Web technologies at: http://sunylanewtechwiki.pbwiki.com

Knowledge Bases

The University of Huddersfield (UK) has created an Electronic Resources Wiki that guides users to information and documentation for using their electronic databases at: http://library.hud.ac.uk/wiki, and the Princeton (NJ) Public Library provides book reviews within genres ranging from contemporary fiction to westerns on its BookLover's Wiki at: http://booklovers.pbwiki.com

HOW ARE LIBRARIANS USING WIKIS?

Librarians—organizers and disseminators of information by nature—have embraced wiki technology in their endeavor to capture and provide knowledge to their patrons and each other. Librarians are creating readers' advisories, LIS encyclopedias, guides to local information, collections of library instruction resources, and directories of blogging librarians.

Library Success Wiki
www.libsuccess.org

The Library Success Wiki is a best practices wiki for the field of library and information science. It is a place for libraries and information professionals to share their ideas, materials, and success stories pertaining to the library discipline. Categories cover a gamut of LIS topics, such as "Management and Leadership," "Selling Your Library," and "Programming." Contributors do not

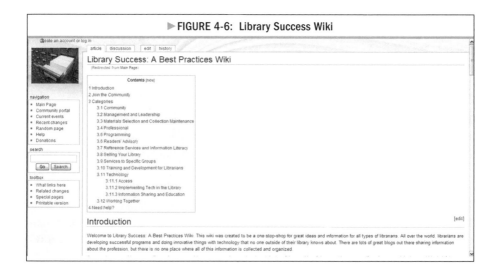

▶ FIGURE 4-6: Library Success Wiki

need to register to participate in the Library Success community, although nearly 200 have done so.

WIKI SOFTWARE

Much like blogging software, there are two kinds of wiki software: hosted and self-hosted. Hosted wiki solutions—often referred to as wiki farms—are maintained by a service provider and offer their users a quick way to initiate a wiki community. Those that must be installed and hosted by the user often offer additional functionality and features, as well as added control and flexibility.

PBWiki

http://pbwiki.com

With over 150,000 hosted wikis, PBWiki is one of the world's largest consumer wiki farms. It offers its users unlimited pages on public or password-protected private wikis. It allows file uploads and attachments and provides RSS feeds, .zip backups, and user commenting. It also provides a WYSIWYG editor with plug-ins enabling wiki creators to add calendars, chat rooms, and more to their wikis.

JotSpot

www.jotspot.com

Owned by Google, JotSpot is a hosted wiki application targeting business users. Users can create corporate intranets using JotSpot's robust suite of Web-based tools such as spreadsheets, calendars, blogs, photo galleries, and documents. It offers a WYSIWYG editor, the ability to import Word documents as wiki pages, and the capacity to e-mail comments directly to the wiki.

SocialText

www.socialtext.com

SocialText is the leading enterprise wiki solution that is used for collaboration by over 2,000 organizations. Wiki creators are provided with a WYSIWYG editor, the ability to e-mail content to any page, advanced access control, and RSS feeds. Intel's Suite Two Enterprise Suite has integrated the SocialText wiki along with the Six Apart Blog, News Gator RSS aggregator, and Simple Feed's feed publishing technology.

Mediawiki

www.mediawiki.org/wiki/MediaWiki

Originally developed to power the well-known Wikipedia, MediaWiki is an open-source, free software package licensed under the GNU General Public License (GPL). One of the most popular wiki engines, it is utilized by all Wikimedia Foundation wikis as well as the Wikia community. Additional to the basic set of wiki features, MediaWiki offers an array of extensions that expand its functionality, such as the Google Maps and PayPal tools.

Wetpaint

www.wetpaint.com

A Seattle-based startup, Wetpaint hosts over 300,000 user-created public wikis. Wetpaint users can include photos, video, calendars, and user comments in their wikis. It offers a WYSIWYG editor, RSS feeds, site activity reports, access control, and tagging.

Wikispaces

www.wikispaces.com

Owned by San Francisco-based Tangient, this wiki farm provides a free and easy way to create public wikis. It offers wiki creators unlimited pages, a WYSIWYG editor, .zip backups, RSS feeds, tags, and an editable left navigation bar. Users can embed photos, audio, or video into their wikispaces.

To compare these and many other Wikis, create a custom wiki comparison matrix at: www.wikimatrix.org

BLOGS VS. WIKIS

Wikis and blogs are similar in that they are both powerful content management systems capable of producing valuable information resources, but there are some key differences between the two.

▶TABLE 4-1: Blogs vs. Wikis	
Blogs	**Wikis**
Chronological: Blog Posts are stamped with the time and date of their creation and are organized with the most recent appearing at the top of the blog.	**Iterative:** Users make edits and changes to a constantly evolving creation.
Individual Creation: The community is invited to participate through comments.	**Community Creation:** Individuals contribute to the work as a whole.
Organized Structure: Blogs have a fixed organizational scheme by date, with older posts sent to archives.	**Organic Structure:** Users contribute to both the main content and the organizational structure of wikis.
Useful for Conversation: Blogs offer a chance for a back-and-forth dialogue with the community.	**Useful for Collaboration:** Wikis are most useful for cooperating on a task or project, saving opinions and random musings for a separate discussion/comments arena.
Permanent: Usually, blog posts and/or their contents are not deleted or even edited.	**Ever-changing:** Wikis are in a constant state of change, growing with their community.
Individual Ownership: The blog's author is the owner of all blog content.	**Group Ownership:** The community is the creator and owner of the content of a wiki.

BEST PRACTICES

▶ **Create a Navigational Structure**. Make it easy for your readers by creating a menu system that will allow them to easily navigate your wiki pages. The menu should be clearly visible and available to users on each page of the wiki or at least on the main "Home" page.

▶ **Seed the Wiki**. An empty wiki is too intimidating for most users to approach; make your wiki more welcoming by stocking it with starter content. If you are creating a book review wiki, post several reviews to get users going; if you are developing a staff wiki, create departmental pages that can be edited by employees.

▶ **Establish a Mission Statement and Usage Policy**. People need guidelines for participating in a wiki, not only to let them know about acceptable usage, but also about the main objectives of the project. What is the purpose of the wiki? What are the main goals you are trying to achieve? Policies such as these are your opportunity to let users know about the direction you would like to see the wiki take, as well as what types of content you hope they will contribute.

▶ **Create an FAQ Section**. Save yourself the time and inconvenience of answering redundant e-mail queries by creating a Frequently Asked Questions page on your wiki. This document will lead collaborators through the steps of contributing to the wiki. Here is where you can combine technical direction with your preferred workflow process. For example, a book review wiki could offer instruction on how to utilize the software to add a new wiki page, but also the steps they would like the contributor to take in order to add a new book review, such as also adding a biographical page for the author.

▶ **Utilize Permission Levels**. Most wikis have the capacity to allow administrators to add user types with varying permission levels, and wiki creators should take advantage of this feature. If you want your wiki to be public but do not want readers to be able to make changes to it, set the permission levels accordingly. If you want others to be able to contribute and edit, but not be able to delete pages, assign them limited rights. These permissions settings enable administrators to completely control access to their wiki.

▶ **Track Changes**. As the wiki author, you will want to keep abreast of what is happening with your wiki at all times. Most wikis will allow creators to keep updated on any and all changes, edits, or deletions to the wiki as soon as they are made. Some wikis offer this feature upon sign-in, while others offer RSS feeds to keep authors notified.

(Cont'd.)

BEST PRACTICES *(Continued)*

▶ **Be Aware of Spammers**. Just as on blogs, spammers sometimes post irrelevant content on wikis, which must be removed. By tracking and monitoring recent changes to the wiki, administrators will be able to catch most of this activity; there also are plugins and spam filters available that wiki authors may install in order to block spammers' efforts.

▶ **Create Regular Backups**. If you are creating a permanent online resource, such as a subject guide or digital resource collection, you will want to make an effort to create regular backups of your data. Most wikis offer this functionality as either a backup or export option.

▶ **Market Your Wiki**. There are many ways to publicize your wiki resource, including press releases, virtual events, announcing it on your library Web site and on all social networking profiles, and linking to it on your blog. In addition, new wiki authors may want to approach bloggers who have an interest in the subject matter and ask them to announce the resource.

REFERENCE

Levine, Robert. 2006. "New Web Sites Seeking Profit in Wiki Model." *New York Times* (September 4): C1.

►5

SOCIAL BOOKMARKING

Technological advancements accompanying the new Web have brought along with them a movement toward organizing data in the public sphere. Consequently, these innovations have brought about the pioneering development of discovery systems. Unlike social networking sites like MySpace and Facebook, which prioritize developing relationships, social bookmarking Web sites focus on managing and sharing information. As users arrange, sort, and share their data in these social settings, they collectively create a repository of user-recommended resources and potentially likeminded people to be explored by the populace. These discovery networks emphasize browsing rather than searching in hopes that people will stumble upon serendipitous resources in the course of their journeys.

Social bookmarking applications such as del.icio.us and Furl allow members to bookmark Web sites, articles, blog posts, podcasts, images, and other Web-based materials for future retrieval in an online space. Since these "favorites" are not stored locally, they become accessible from any online computer instead of being limited to the user's desktop. By saving and storing bookmarks within one of these Web site communities, favorites become not only portable and searchable, but public and social as well, with the capacity to be browsed by others looking to discover new resources.

Bookmark collections are organized by members who assign descriptive keywords or tags to categorize each item, allowing for a self-service taxonomy. Members' tags are also added to the community tag pool to create a folksonomy, a naturally created classification system that arises as a result of user-based tagging. Within these Web sites, people can navigate by either tags or other bookmarkers.

The simple brilliance and ease of use of social bookmarking Web sites has led them to become a Web 2.0 phenomenon. The leader in this space, del.icio.us, has been acquired by the Yahoo! network and enjoys over 1.5 million registered users. Bookmarking has tipped from being a geek-only pastime to adoption by a mass audience. Average Web users are bookmarking sites they want to remember later, students are creating portable bibliographies, educators are creating course reading lists, and distributed researchers are collaborating on projects.

The social networking giant, Facebook has developed within its academic ecosystem its own social bookmarking functionality that allows members to bookmark and share Internet resources with selected friends. IBM has enabled a community of more than 6,000 employees to create a collection of 100,000 bookmarks reflecting their corporate culture with Dogear, their own in-house bookmarking program. Corporations and businesses today have begun to implement this practice of intranet bookmarking, allowing project teams and executives alike to create communities of expertise within the safety of their firewall.

Major online publications are responding to their readers' proclivity for saving items for future use by integrating links and shortcuts to popular social bookmarking sites as options with each article. *Sports Illustrated* enables regular visitors to save stories within their own social bookmaking service, as well as to share them through Facebook. *The Washington Post* offers its readers shortcuts to bookmark articles within their del.icio.us, Facebook, Yahoo!, or Google Bookmarks accounts. *The New York Times* online edition facilitates saving and sharing stories through Facebook as well as social news sites Digg and Newsvine. This Web 2.0 trend will continue to gain steam as the general public becomes increasingly more aware of the advantages of saving, storing, and sharing their favorite resources in a way that is portable, sortable, and searchable.

INSIDE SOCIAL BOOKMARKING

Although each social bookmarking application varies in design appearance, there are certain features that are shared by the majority of these programs.

Bookmarklets are quick-save shortcut buttons that are installed on the Web browser. They allow new Web site resources to be added to a user's collection with a click. When users post a new item with a bookmarklet, they are offered a form in which the Web site title and URL have been provided. Bookmarkers can supply tags to be assigned to that item, as well as descriptive notes.

Bookmarks are Web-based resources that have been added to a user's collection. They are each displayed with the tags that have been assigned to them, along with user notes or descriptions and the number of other users who have also bookmarked that item.

Tags are descriptive keywords that people can assign to their bookmarks in order to organize and remember them later. As new items are added, recommended tags are often suggested to the user based on those they have previously used, or those that are popular keywords used by others who have bookmarked the same item. Tags offer an alternate form of navigation within a user's own collection

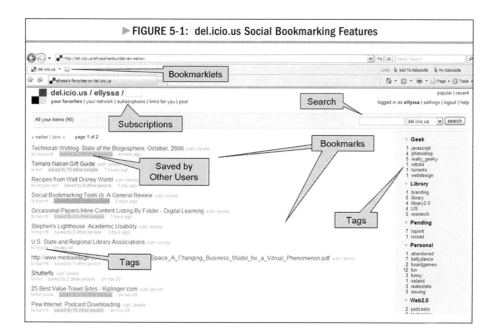

▶FIGURE 5-1: del.icio.us Social Bookmarking Features

of bookmarks, as well as the Web site community as a whole. Some of these communities allow their users to subscribe to tags, updating them when any member of the community adds a new bookmark that is described with a particular keyword.

Saved by Other Users is a feature offered by most of these programs, which enables users to view all of the other people who have saved a particular item, as well as the tags they used to describe it and any user notes they may have added. This allows bookmarkers to navigate by user to discover new resources. Users often are able to subscribe to other users who share their areas of interest, in order to keep updated as that bookmarker adds new items.

Search enables users to conduct queries within their own set of bookmarks, as well as within the larger collection of the community.

Subscriptions, often called watchlists, allow people to subscribe to other bookmarkers and sometimes even tags within the community. Additionally, RSS feeds are provided for every page within these communities, enabling people to subscribe to users and tags through their news readers.

The **Global Tag Cloud** is a representation of the most popular tags in use by a Web site community at any given time. This cloud will aggregate and display the more popular tags in larger text and bolder fonts, offering people insight into what is currently in public favor at any particular time. This textual display is also a form of navigation, allowing people to browse and discover bookmarks tagged with a particular keyword.

▶FIGURE 5-2: del.icio.us Global Tag Cloud

HOW ARE LIBRARIES USING SOCIAL BOOKMARKING?

Libraries are using social bookmarking applications to provide patrons with subject guides, recommended Web resources lists, and reader's advisory sources. They are bookmarking Web sites, images, and podcasts in subject areas ranging from business to baseball and offering their patrons an up-to-the-minute guide to the best of the Web. Librarians are collaborating with colleagues to save and share relevant resources to keep updated on the latest library literature and technology news. Here is a look at some of the inventive ways libraries are utilizing this new technology.

University of Pennsylvania's Penn Tags
http://tags.library.upenn.edu/

In the summer of 2005, the librarians at the University of Pennsylvania Libraries joined to create PennTags, a customized social bookmarking community for their students, faculty, and staff. PennTags was devised by Mike Winkler, Director of Information Technology & Digital Development, and Laurie Allen, Social Science Data Services Librarian, as a way for librarians to create subject guides on the Web and for faculty to author dynamic annotated bibliographies. "We liked the idea of having a space for academics in the social bookmarking world," said Allen.

Through the PennTags system, community members may create bookmarks for any Web content, including library resources. Bookmarks may include records from the library OPAC, full-text journal articles, and items from their video catalog, as well as any e-resource or database. Members can make their favorites public or private and have the ability to segregate them into projects.

The librarians had previously used the del.icio.us bookmarking service, but chose to build their own in order to integrate it with their library catalog and gain

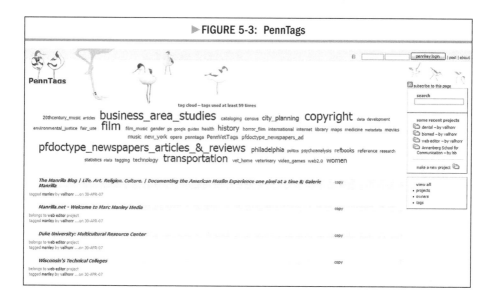

▶ **FIGURE 5-3:** PennTags

further flexibility. They built the current version of PennTags using an Oracle database, Perl, and SQL due to their existing skill set in these areas. They decided to use these technologies due to efficiency, as they hoped to produce a proof of concept application swiftly and garner a community response. For the next iteration, they plan to use open-source technology.

Although the library introduced the system to a few faculty members, they did no marketing. The current version, which is still considered pre-launch, has accumulated 13,000 posts and over 800 users. The library plans to make their official launch with much more fanfare.

If they were to do anything differently, the librarians at the UPL would have chronicled their progress for the public within a project blog. Allen advises other libraries to "just go for it." She tells others who are considering such an undertaking to learn from their users and to not be afraid to put out an unfinished product. "Whatever you can do, just give it to your patrons and see what they say," Allen recommends. (Laurie Allen, telephone conversation with author, March 2007)

Other Ways Libraries Are Using Social Bookmarking

Subject Guides

The Lansing (IL) Public Library has collected over 600 bookmarked resources in subject areas ranging from travel and women's history to parenting, and politics at: http://del.icio.us/lansingpubliclibrary, and the San Mateo (CA) Public Library's over 400 bookmarks are arranged and tagged according to the Dewey classification system at: http://del.icio.us/SanMateoLibrary

Resource Collections

The Washington State Library collects federal and state government resources through their del.cio.us bookmarks at: http://del.icio.us/wastatelib

Keeping Current

The librarians at the Maui (HI) Community College Library stay up to date with the latest in computer technologies, such as JavaScript and AJAX, with their bookmarks at: http://del.icio.us/mauicclibrary and social bookmarking is used to keep current with recent developments with the Web, gadgets, and computer technology at the Thomas Ford Memorial Library (Western Springs, IL) at: http://del.icio.us/thomasford. The librarians at the Carl A. Pescosolido Library, the Governor's Academy (Byfield, MA) are using del.icio.us to keep track of recent library 2.0 resources at: http://del.icio.us/peskylibrary

Reader's Advisory

The staff of the Courtney Park branch of the Mississauga (ON, Canada) Public Library use their social bookmarking account to store their favorite children's and reader's advisory resources at: http://del.icio.us/crtstaff

Staff Resources

The Seldovia (AK) Public Library bookmarks resources related to library operations, outreach, and collection development at: http://del.icio.us/seldovia.library

Web Site Gadgets

The Lakeland Campus (FL) Library syndicates their del.icio.us links on the sidebar of their library Web page at: http://catherin.blog.usf.edu

HOW ARE LIBRARIANS USING SOCIAL BOOKMARKING?

Librarians are using social bookmarking tools to organize their personal research by subject area, to track conference-related materials, and to keep up with developments in the field. They are posting and saving journal articles, PowerPoint presentations, podcasts, and blog posts for later retrieval and are sharing with and subscribing to fellow colleagues and noteworthy tags.

The "library2.0" Tag

www.stumbleupon.com/tag/library2.0

The library field has come to know the term library2.0 as a designation representing the movement toward user involvement in the design of library services and offerings. Over the past year, there has been a wealth of information made available online concerning this topic in the form of blog posts, journal articles, podcasts, conference presentations, images, and case studies. Librarians who have been following this

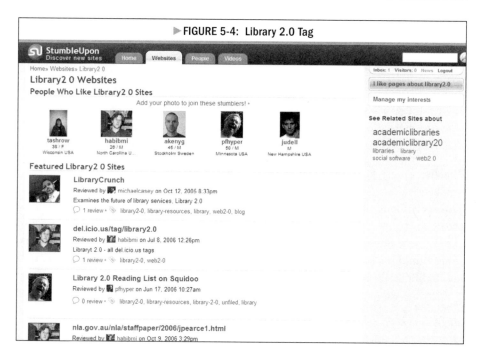

▷ FIGURE 5-4: Library 2.0 Tag

discussion have made use of social bookmarking tools to save relevant resources about this new concept, and they have tagged them with the descriptive keyword: "library2.0." This agreement on a common tag has made these bookmarking Web sites terrific research sources, as people can easily click on the tag to view every resource that has been thus tagged. A search for the term "library2.0" on del.icio.us alone yields over 6,300 results. Incidentally, a tag search such as this one also can be conducted across other new social Web sites such as Flickr (photos), Technorati(blogs), and YouTube (videos), to name a few. And for many of today's library conferences, a shared tag, such as CIL2007 or ALA2007, will be posted most often on the conference wiki. All related materials, such as bookmarks, videos, photos, and text, will be tagged identically within these Web 2.0 sites, making it easy to find indexed content.

SOCIAL BOOKMARKING TOOLS

del.icio.us
http://del.icio.us

Owned by Yahoo!, del.icio.us is the most recognized social bookmarking application, with over 1.5 million users. In addition to the basic set of features, users have the ability to bookmark items for other people, create a network of friends, and subscribe to both people and tags. del.icio.us users can also organize their tags into hierarchical tag bundles.

Furl

www.furl.net

LookSmart's Furl is a bookmarking service that provides its members with a wide range of useful features. One exceptional feature offered by Furl is Web page caching. Instead of linking to Web resources as users bookmark them, the program saves a full copy of each page, which is added to a member's 5 GB of storage space. Members have the ability to export their bookmarks in the form of a .zip archive, as well as export them to bibliographic software programs such as BibTex or Endnote.

Blinklist

www.blinklist.com

This social bookmarking tool offers its members the capability to rate bookmarks, create and share with friends lists, import bookmarks from other services, and export personal tag clouds to any blog or Web site. When members post an item using Blinklist's bookmarklet button, the program will take any text that the user has highlighted on a Web page and autofill it into the description field of the form.

Magnolia

http://ma.gnolia.com

Magnolia has implemented some of the best features of the leading bookmarking services. Its members can rate bookmarks, create contacts, make bookmarks private, and view a global tag cloud. Additionally, Magnolia saves full copies of Web pages for members and allows them to form organized groups in which individuals contribute to the collective pool of bookmarks.

StumbleUpon

www.stumbleupon.com

With over 2.2 million users, StumbleUpon rivals del.icio.us for the title of the most popular social bookmarking tool available. This browser plug-in for Internet Explorer or Firefox enables people to discover new Web sites by clicking on the Stumble button. People can rate and review Web resources, create organized groups, share with friends' networks, and get personalized recommendations while surfing the Internet. This discovery tool was acquired by eBay in May 2007.

ACADEMIC SOCIAL BOOKMARKING APPLICATIONS

Academic social bookmarking applications are a subset, or variety, of the newly popularized Web 2.0 bookmarking tools. These applications are aimed at researchers. Instead of "favoriting" a Web page or video, bookmarkers using these tools collect citation information for journal articles and other resources. They enable students, scholars, and researchers to bookmark and organize their references into comprehensive online bibliographies. Through these free services, people can search bibliographic databases to retrieve journal articles, conference proceedings, theses, and reports. Academics may categorize their articles and items by assigning descriptive tag words to them. Many of these applications produce records that can be exported to traditional reference management software programs such as Endnote and BibTex.

A CiteULike Quicktake

www.citeulike.org

The CiteULike application has been created as a tool to facilitate the organization of academic research in a way that is portable and social. Researchers are able to bookmark scholarly papers and articles, organize their reference libraries, and share them with others in the community.

By utilizing this scholarly bookmarking application, members are able to create detailed bibliographic records for online resources, including volume, issue, and editorial information exportable to both BibTex and Endnote. Citation information is automatically acquired from supported databases, including PubMed, JSTOR, and Ingenta, and may be entered manually for those that are not. Members can tag resources, create watchlists, and join research groups.

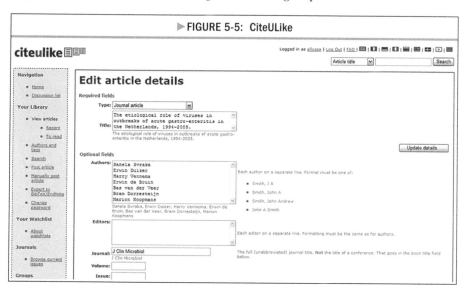

▶ FIGURE 5-5: CiteULike

Other Academic Bookmarking Tools

Connotea

www.connotea.org

Researchers and scientists are active users in this specialized social bookmarking service from the publishers of the *Nature* journal. Connotea automates bookmarking journal articles and Web sites with its bookmarklet, which instantly obtains citation information from various sources, such as BioMed Central, PubMed, and Wiley Interscience.

Zotero
www.zotero.org

Zotero is an extension for Firefox 2.0, which enables browsers to capture citation information from Web pages quickly and easily. Researchers can add searchable notecards to their citations, organize them with tags, attach files to them, arrange them into folders, or export them as formatted citations. Zotero can capture a single citation or an entire results list of sources, which researchers can work with either online or offline.

Complore
http://complore.com

Complore encourages scholars and students to save their lectures, articles, and papers in this bibliographic bookmarking service. Researchers can join groups, subscribe to a site-wide RSS feed, and generate BibTex records.

Bibsonomy
www.bibsonomy.org

Created by the Knowledge and Data Engineering Group at the University of Kassel, Germany, Bibsonomy is a scholarly bookmarking service that offers its users related tags, the ability to create groups, and the ability to export records to BibTex. Bibsonomy members can construct friends networks, import their del.icio.us links, generate private entries, and import their BibTex libraries.

BEST PRACTICES

▶ **Decide on One Tag.** If you want to establish a standard tag for general use for a course reading list, a conference, or event, decide on one tag to describe all related resources, such as LIS901-06 or CIL2008, and then stick with it. Although you can also use other descriptors, such as "upcoming" or "library," you will want to publicize one particular tag for everyone to use when both describing and searching for your event. Continue to tag relevant items with that descriptor across all Web 2.0 applications you frequent, such as in your blog posts, Flickr photos, YouTube videos, etc.

▶ **Tag as a Reader Would.** If you are tagging items for others on a social bookmarking Web site, think about describing resources from the user's perspective. Use the tag "readers_advisory" if your target user group consists of fellow librarians on your staff, but use the term "book_recommendations" if your users include the general public.

▶ **Organize Tags into Bundles.** Keep your tags organized by placing them into bundles, particularly if you are using del.icio.us. Bundles are groupings of tags or tag headings that are similar to folders. Tags may be placed into multiple bundles at the same time.

▶ **Weed Your Collection.** It is just as important to weed outdated items in an online resources collection as it is in a print one. Take a look at your oldest bookmarks to see which ones you have not accessed in several months, or which links are no longer working.

▶ **Cross-Market.** Take advantage of this public and social venue to cross-market your other online efforts. Bookmark your blog, a couple of your hot posts, your wiki, etc. You will be able to view how many other people have bookmarked them also.

▶ **Market Yourself!** If you are bookmarking for public consumption, make your user name public along with which community you are using, so that your patrons can look you up and add you to their networks. Post about your bookmarks on your blog, add a link on your library's Web site, etc. If you are organizing a conference or event, be sure to include your preferred tag on your promotional materials such as a conference-planning wiki, Web page, pens, or other schwag you plan to give away, etc.

▶6

PHOTO SHARING

I n the age of the new Web, online photo sharing has become a booming phenomenon with no signs of fading. Yahoo! now indexes over three billion photos online. Trained photographers and everyday shutterbugs are uploading their work with fervor. Users are rating, reviewing, annotating, and "favoriting" each other's images. They are searching, browsing, tagging, and creating a wealth of personal, cultural, and historical digital image collections.

Through photo-sharing sites such as Flickr, PhotoBucket, and Webshots, users can now access their digital image collections remotely from any Web-enabled device that will support them. They can also browse the photos of others, many of which are reusable under Creative Commons licenses. These Web sites have become talent wells, brimming with undiscovered skill and potential, and savvy corporations are taking note. Businesses such as Nikon are going to the source to stock their advertising campaigns, such as the one at: www.stunningnikon.com/dslr/in which Flickr users were given new Nikon DSLR cameras in exchange for their photos.

The concept of storing and managing digital images online is not a new one. The innovation of Web 2.0 digital image management lies in the notion of *sharing* this content with other people and allowing user interaction. This new cadre of image-sharing applications embraces the social nature of the participatory Web, connecting people to people not just with information. These programs are an exemplar of the network effect, as their pool of images gain in value as they increase in quantity and this value is an afterthought of those who contribute to it.

There are a slew of new photo-sharing applications available today. Up to two million images a day are uploaded to Flickr alone, which lays claim to a total of over 500 million digital photos (Graham, 2007). Although some may boast more users, Flickr is ahead of the pack when it comes to Web 2.0 features. Flickr's recipe for success consists of equal parts online photo storage and image management, combined with two parts social functionality. Through Flickr, users are not only sharing their digital images with their family, friends, and contacts, but they are joining groups, commenting on photos, subscribing via RSS feeds, and tagging images. Here is a look at some of Flickr's forward-thinking features, such as clustered search terms and geotagging, that have established the company as a thought leader in this space.

PHOTO SHARING FEATURES

Flickr was conceived to be a social application and was built with those characteristics from the ground up. Right now, Flickr is the photo-sharing Web site with the most social features; however, other online photo storage programs are moving quickly to adopt similar functionality.

Contacts are people with whom users have established a connection. Flickr members can differentiate between these connections by classifying them according to how well they know them. People can be added and invited by others as family, friends, or contacts. Users can set permission levels for each of their photos, which will determine which groups of people—if any—are allowed to view them.

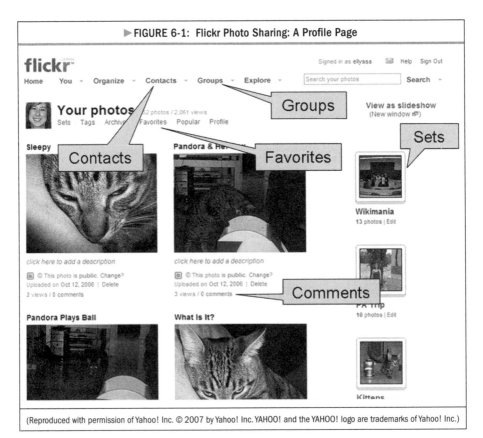

▶ FIGURE 6-1: Flickr Photo Sharing: A Profile Page

(Reproduced with permission of Yahoo! Inc. © 2007 by Yahoo! Inc. YAHOO! and the YAHOO! logo are trademarks of Yahoo! Inc.)

Sets are groups of images that have been gathered together into subsets of the member's photo collection. Similar to separate folders containing like items, sets are a useful way to organize and arrange photos related to a specific event, place, or person. Sets are created by the user and can relate to such things as wedding photos, a recent trip, a business conference, photos of a favorite pet, a new haircut, and so on.

Groups are mini forums for people with similar interests to share their images and discuss related topics. After members have uploaded their photos, they have the option to send them to any of the groups to which they belong. The photos that they opt to send are posted to the group's main pool of images, while at the same time remaining in the member's album. Groups can range in size and scope from those that welcome newbies, such as "FlickrCentral" with over 43,000 members, to the highly focused "Beach Photography" group that holds monthly photography contests for their 7,000 members, to the "just for fun" groups such as the "Cats in Sinks" and "Dogs Eating Potato Chips" groups, which have 400 members combined.

▶FIGURE 6-2: Flickr Photo Sharing: Features on Individual Photo Page

(Reproduced with permission of Yahoo! Inc. © 2007 by Yahoo! Inc. YAHOO! and the YAHOO! logo are trademarks of Yahoo! Inc.)

Favorites are images that are preferred by a user. The member bookmarks them for easy retrieval at a future time. Any publicly viewable image may be added to a user's Favorites folder. In turn, image owners can view how many users have bookmarked each of their photos as Favorites and who each of those members are.

Comments are an opportunity for members to share brief opinions about a photograph. This social feature shares the same functionality as comments left on blog posts. Comments can be left on any public image by completing a brief form below it.

Tags are descriptive keywords that members assign to their images. Consequently, users are able to create a personalized classification system for their photos, as well as contribute to the Web site's overall folksonomy. As in other social software applications, Flickr has a global tag cloud displaying the most popular tags currently in use, and allows members to navigate and search by tag. Clicking on a tag within a member's collection will return all of their photos that they have tagged with that particular keyword, as well as the choice to view all photos throughout the community, which have been tagged accordingly.

Annotations are short notes that can be left directly on an image. Members select the "Add Note" tool and simply drag and resize a rectangular box to create a "hotspot" that will pop up a note when moused over. Art History teachers are already using this useful feature as a teaching tool for highlighting techniques and artistic theory as in an image of a Renaissance painting at: http://flickr.com/photos/hal12/234233755/ or http://tinyurl.com/2s4mjy

Clustered Tag Searching is an extension of the ability to navigate and search by tag. While one of the benefits of a tag-based classification system is the lack of restrictions placed on the user when determining appropriate tags, one of its weaknesses is its lack of hierarchical structure. The inclusive nature of a tagging system, which allows users to capture all nuances of concepts and language, also makes it difficult to find items through searching. As a way to provide some context for tags, Flickr has introduced tag clusters that combine similar tags into meaningful clusters. For instance, a search for the tag "apple" will return thousands of results. Tag clusters help organize these results into subset clusters that are sorted by the term "apple" as it pertains to: the red fruit, the MacIntosh computer, the MacIntosh operating system, and the Big Apple—New York City.

Geotagging is the feature that allows members to associate their photos with the place where they were taken. Users can drag and drop their photos onto a detailed Yahoo! map, which can also be viewed as a satellite image. Map information becomes linked to photos that have been geotagged. This feature is so popular with Flickr users that over 1.2 million photos were geotagged within the first 24 hours of its introduction.

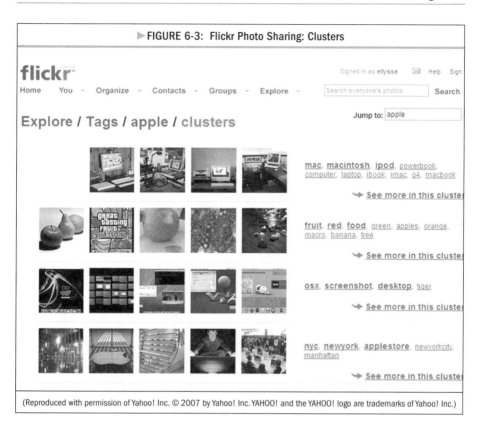

▶ FIGURE 6-3: Flickr Photo Sharing: Clusters

(Reproduced with permission of Yahoo! Inc. © 2007 by Yahoo! Inc. YAHOO! and the YAHOO! logo are trademarks of Yahoo! Inc.)

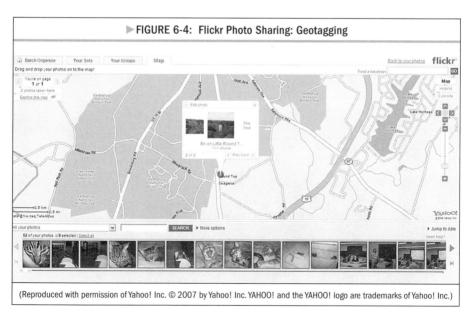

▶ FIGURE 6-4: Flickr Photo Sharing: Geotagging

(Reproduced with permission of Yahoo! Inc. © 2007 by Yahoo! Inc. YAHOO! and the YAHOO! logo are trademarks of Yahoo! Inc.)

HOW ARE LIBRARIES USING PHOTO SHARING?

Libraries are finding photo-sharing applications useful for marketing efforts and community outreach as well as for digital image management. They have begun posting photos of new books, library events, and guided tours, as well as images of library staff and volunteers. These examples demonstrate some of the more innovative possibilities with such social applications.

The Palos Verdes Library District's 40 Families Project
www.40families.org
In September of 2004, the Palos Verdes Library District undertook a project to discover the identities of some 40 families who appeared within a three-foot-long photograph taken in 1923. The photograph depicts local Japanese farmers from the Palos Verdes Peninsula, who had gathered to celebrate the opening of a community hall. Hoping to tell the stories of these early residents, Project Manager David Campbell teamed up with a local history librarian and area residents to solve the mystery of the photo.

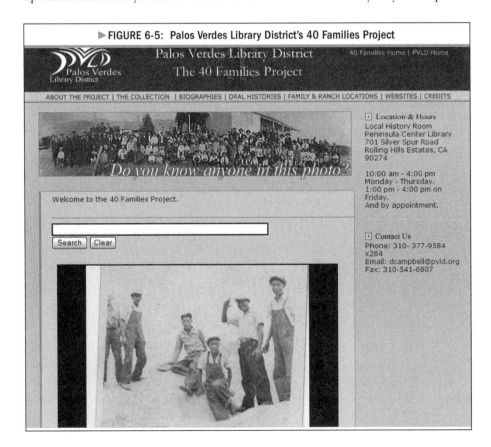

▶ FIGURE 6-5: Palos Verdes Library District's 40 Families Project

The library research team sought to identify the members of the photo, as well as to paint a picture of their daily lives through oral histories, ascertain the original locations of their farms on a map of the peninsula, and to create a special local history "Japanese American Collection" to be housed by the Peninsula Center Library.

In order to gain exposure for the project, the group chose to use the Flickr photo-sharing Web site, which not only publicized the endeavor, but also facilitated an annotated slideshow within the main 40 Families Web site. "It gave us some cool tricks for incorporating the images into the project Web site. Flickr was so popular we ended up using it in our Learning 2.0 project and teens Web site," said Campbell.

Campbell's team learned that most of the area's Japanese American population was sent to the Poston camp in Arizona during World War II. In the spirit of the 40 Families Project, the PVLD hosted the 2006 reunion of the Poston camp, garnering the largest turnout the event has had in years. "The project reached an apex then, because we realized we were giving information back to the community," commented Campbell.

Over 150 photos from the era have been donated to the project, which has collected original documents, magazine and newspaper articles, biographies, microfilm, and oral histories. With the help of the community, the project has managed to determine the identities of more than 70 percent of the photo's subjects and has plotted the locations of over 40 farms and ranches on a map.

Campbell hopes to integrate a Google map into the project's Web site and mash it up with their Flickr collection, along with a content management system. The team is very happy with the Flickr technology and would reuse it. Campbell offers this advice to others who are planning a project such as this one: have a good system for tracking and collecting data and have someone on your team who knows project management. (David Campbell, e-mail correspondence with author, March 2007)

Other Ways Libraries Are Using Photo Sharing

Marketing and Promotion

The Colorado College Tutt Library provides images of READ posters and library signs at: www.flickr.com/photos/tuttlibrary, while the Dublin City (Ireland) Public Library spotlights their library publications within their Flickr profile at: www.flickr.com/photos/dublincitypubliclibraries. The ASU Libraries at Arizona State University show off their library staff in their photo collections at: www.flickr.com/photos/asulibraries

Patrons

The American Library Association is showing off their events and volunteers at: www.flickr.com/photos/ala_members, and the Asheboro (NC) Public Library displays photos of its library patrons at: www.flickr.com/photos/asheborolibrary

New Acquisitions

The Westmont (IL) Public Library displays new titles in their photos at: www.flickr. com/photos/westmontlibrary and links to their Flickr account on their Web site at: http://westmontlibrary.org

Special Collections and Exhibits

The Weymouth (MA) Public Library collects local historical photos at: www.flickr. com/photos/wpl, and banned book displays are spotlighted in the photos of the Newport (OR) Public Library at: www.flickr.com/photos/newport publiclibrary

Outreach

The Homer Township (IL) Public Library promotes outreach efforts, such as their bookmobile, at: www.flickr.com/photos/homerlibrary

Special Events

The Meeteetse (WY) Branch Library photographs the parties and events at their library at: www.flickr.com/photos/meeteetselibrary while author events are captured by the Waterloo (ON, Canada) Public Library at: www.flickr.com/photos/waterloo public library. The Gwinnett County (ON, Canada)Public Library provides images of their "Rock the Shelves" library concert at: www.flickr.com/photos/gwinnett countypubliclibrary; the Kenton County (KY) Public Library offers images of its Scrabble Game Night at: www.flickr.com/photos/kentonlibrary; and the Mt. Lebanon (PA) Public Library provides photos from its Read-to-Me Party at: www.flickr.com/photos/mtlebanonlibrary

Library Building

The Lackman (KS) Library has created a photographic virtual tour at: www.flickr.com/ photos/11329886@N00 and the construction and renovation activities are documented by the Tipton (IN) Public Library at: www.flickr.com/photos/tipton publiclibrary

Library Programming

The St. Joseph County (IN) Public Library keeps a photographic record of their gaming nights at: www.flickr.com/photos/sjcpl while the Buckham Memorial Library (Faribault, MN) provides images of their puppet, juggler, and storytime programs at: www.flickr.com/photos/buckhamlibrary. The Worthington (OH) Libraries highlight their Summer Reading and Touch A Truck programs at: www.flickr.com/photos/ coollibrary and the music and storytime events are photographed at the Marathon County (WI) Public Library at: www.flickr.com/ photos/mcpl

Staff Training

The Michigan Library Consortium offers images of its training workshops and annual meetings at: www.flickr.com/photos/michiganlibraryconsortium

HOW ARE LIBRARIANS USING PHOTO SHARING?

Librarians are using social photo-sharing applications, such as Flickr, to collect and organize library-related photos and share them with others in the field. They are joining groups such as those dedicated to READ posters, Librarian Trading Cards, and Library Signage.

Libraries and Librarians Flickr Group

http://www.flickr.com/groups/librariesandlibrarians

Over 1,500 librarians have joined the Libraries and Librarians Group on Flickr. Within the group, librarians are uploading and sharing images of libraries, librarians, conferences, workshops, events, displays, Web sites, and virtual worlds. The group's main photo pool contains over 9,000 images. Librarians from across the globe connect in this group to discuss emerging technology trends and libraries.

▶ FIGURE 6-6: Libraries and Librarians Group

(Reproduced with permission of Yahoo! Inc. © 2007 by Yahoo! Inc. YAHOO! and the YAHOO! logo are trademarks of Yahoo! Inc.)

PHOTO-SHARING APPLICATIONS

The photo-sharing market is crowded and diverse. Some applications have chosen to focus on image hosting while others are bringing out community features. Some image hosting applications have made themselves major competitors by piggy-backing on the popularity of larger sites, such as MySpace. Photobucket in particular boasts over 41 million members, and 56 percent of its traffic comes from this social networking giant.

Photobucket
http://photobucket.com
This free image and video hosting site allows users to create slideshows and share their images on social networking sites such as MySpace and Facebook. Members can also link to images in e-mail and instant messengers. Photobucket was purchased by MySpace in May 2007.

Webshots
www.webshots.com
Webshots allows users to upload and share up to 1,000 photos with a free account, as well as publish their images to their blog or Web site. Members can explore the community by ten channels of interest such as: entertainment, home & garden, family, sports, and travel.

Kodak Gallery
www.kodakgallery.com
Previously known as Ofoto, the Kodak EasyShare Gallery has over 20 million members. The Web site provides online photo hosting, the ability to edit and

▶TABLE 6-1: Comparison of Web 2.0 Social Features in Photo-Sharing Applications									
	Marketshare	Groups	Tags	RSS Feeds	Comments	Contacts	Favorites	Notes	GeoTagging
Photobucket	43.84%								
Webshots	8.34%	■		■	■	■	■		
Kodak Gallery	6.52%				■	■	■		
Flickr	5.95%	■	■	■	■	■	■	■	■
Snapfish	4.06%					■	■		
(Statistics from Prescott, 2006.)									

remove red-eye, and add effects and borders. Users can also create and buy a large assortment of products made from their images such as: mugs, cards, aprons, posters, calendars, etc.

Flickr
www.flickr.com

Owned by Yahoo!, this photo-sharing community with over 8.5 million members allows members to navigate by "interestingness," upload and geotag photos, annotate images, join groups, explore by camera type, and apply copyright licenses.

Snapfish
www.snapfish.com

Owned by Hewlett-Packard, this is a photo-storage Web site similar to the Kodak EasyShare Gallery. Its 26 million members can purchase prints as well as many other products created from their images such as: memory books, pillow cases, golf towels, coasters, and playing cards.

BEST PRACTICES

▶ **Spotlight Patrons.** Let everyone know how much fun the patrons are having over at your library. Upload snapshots from game nights, book readings, and other special events. Photo-sharing Web sites are fantastic marketing tools that offer you the chance to put the spotlight on your users.

▶ **Show Off Staff.** New social software tools are a great way to highlight the human side of an institution. Use them to show off your friendly and approachable staff members in photos.

▶ **Organize by Sets.** Photo-sharing Web sites provide many ways to organize your digital images. One way is by grouping them into sets or folders. Use these photo management tools to separate photos from each of your major events, your new book offerings, your renovation and building photos, and your special collections.

▶ **Choose a Creative Commons License.** Let your patrons reuse your photos by choosing a creative commons license that allows sharing.

▶ **Join Groups.** Get you or your library out there and noticed by joining groups, chatting on their message boards, and submitting photos to the collective pool.

REFERENCES

Graham, Jefferson. "Yahoo Photos Going Dark as Flickr Shines On." *USA Today* (May 3, 2007). Available: www.usatoday.com/tech/webguide/2007-05-03-yahoo-photos-flickr_N. htm (accessed May 6, 2007).

Prescott, LeeAnn. "PhotoBucket Leads Photo Sharing Sites; Flickr at #6." *Hitwise US* (June 21, 2006). Available: http://weblogs.hitwise.com/leeann-prescott/2006/06/photobucket_leads_photo_sharin.html (accessed December 10, 2006).

►7

SOCIAL CATALOGING

Traditionally, the cataloging of book and media collections has been an occupation reserved for the library realm. However, a new trend in 2.0 applications has simplified this process, offering organizational bliss to the masses. What was once a precise task undertaken by conscientious librarians utilizing costly and complex software and a strict set of rules has been transformed and injected with a good dose of community. It might be considered social networking for media lovers. This new wave of cataloging sites provides a space where members can catalog their own collections, develop a personal taxonomy, and encounter likeminded people.

Social cataloging Web sites enable users to create personal catalogs of their book, CD, DVD, and game collections, and share them with others. Members are able to write reviews, leave comments, assign tags, and make item ratings, which are combined with media information retrieved from Amazon and libraries worldwide. Cataloging records and functionality vary amongst these networks, with some providing access to MARC records, the U.S. Library of Congress and Dewey call numbers, as well as edition information, and others offering the ability to place items on loan.

In addition to cataloging and creating content, members of these organizational communities can learn about other users who own the same media items and share similar tastes. They also can discover new resources while browsing by tags, books, authors, and other members.

The largest of these social cataloging Web sites, LibraryThing, boasts over 249,000 registered members. It is a book catalog that users actually want to hang out in: one which allows them to aid in its creation as well as interact with other contributors. LibraryThing's collection of 17 million books catalogs more items that the New York Public Library or even that of Harvard University, the second largest library in the U.S.

Cataloging is no longer the sole province of the trained professional. Today's average Web users are organizing and managing their collections through sites such as LibraryThing, Shelfari, Listal, and Gurulib. They are holding book discussions, evaluating DVDs, and voicing their opinions. Together, members are crafting people-powered recommendation systems that are searchable, browsable, and enjoyable to explore.

INSIDE SOCIAL CATALOGING

Social cataloging Web sites vary greatly in features and functionality, each offering its own unique experience. This chapter will offer a closer look at the leader in this space, LibraryThing, as it offers the most Web 2.0 features and has set the bar for its competitors. LibraryThing is a social cataloging application for books only.

The **Catalog View** is the main interface through which members view their library collections. Members can explore their own and others' catalogs in a list format, such as the one shown in Figure 7-1, or as a virtual bookshelf that displays only book covers.

Many of these organizational communities empower users to classify their collections according to personal meaning through the use of **Tags**. Members are permitted to assign these keywords to each of their books in order to describe them for future retrieval. Tags assigned to books by individuals are gathered and displayed as a community tag cloud within the Social Information section of the book's cataloging record. Users are able both to browse and search by tag in order to discover new items and navigate the entire collection.

Ratings may be placed on items using a five-star scale within nearly all social cataloging programs. These individual assessments are aggregated within the Social Information tab of the book record in order to produce a cumulative score for the item as determined by the user community.

► FIGURE 7-1: LibraryThing: A Book Catalog

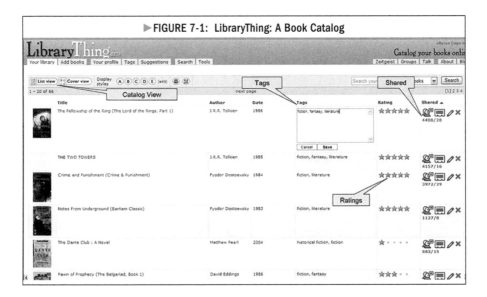

The **Shared** information supplied by most of these applications provides a total number of other users who own a particular item in their library, as well as a complete hyperlinked list of who those people are. This is a powerful social and discovery tool, as it enables the user to browse the collections of those who share their favorite titles.

The **Book Information** section of an item record displays the cataloging information related to the title with minimal social data. This includes publication and edition information, call numbers, subject headings, ISBN numbers, and MARC records.

It is rare to see **Call Numbers** used in these programs; however, both the U.S. Library of Congress and Dewey numbers are provided by LibraryThing with each record.

Editions information, including cover art, ISBN, and purchase information, is offered with each record. Editions are ranked according to popularity.

The **Social Information** section of a cataloging record consists of the user-generated data about that particular item including: user reviews, ratings, members who share that title, tags, and book recommendations. It is from this view that members can gain insight into how others have perceived the book. This view is especially useful for finding book recommendations, as well as other members who share the title.

Reviews can be submitted by individual users within nearly all social cataloging Web sites, and are found listed along with the item's cataloging record.

Recommendations are included in the Social Information section of each cataloging entry. They advise members about which titles they may enjoy based on their like or dislike for the featured book. LibraryThing provides several types of

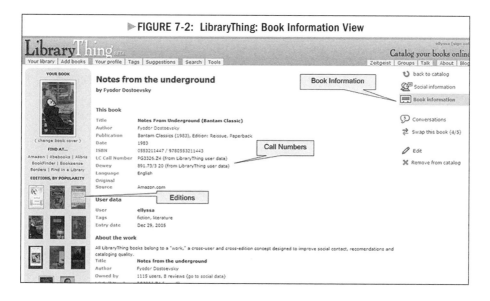

▶FIGURE 7-2: LibraryThing: Book Information View

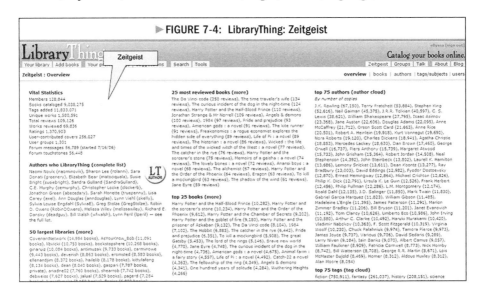

▶ FIGURE 7-3: LibraryThing: Social Information View

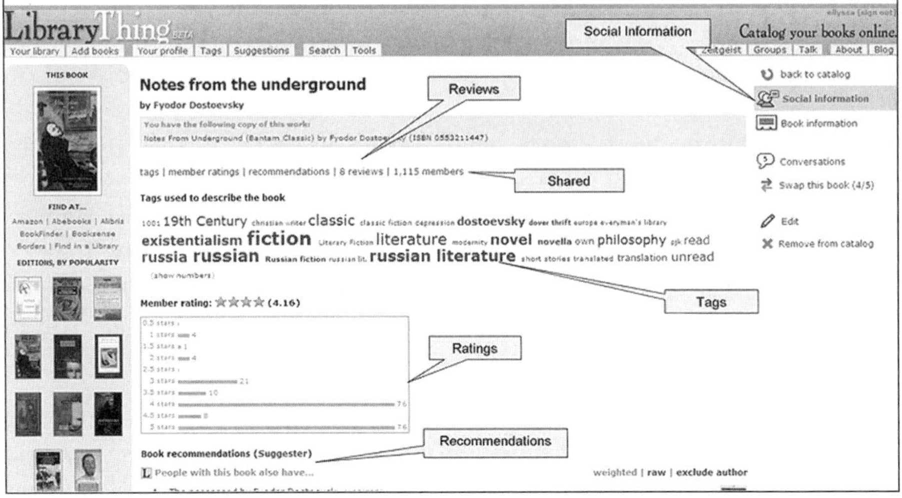

suggestions for readers, including listing the books owned by users who also have the featured title in their library; a list of books with similar tags; a "special sauce" recommendation; Amazon recommendations; and an unsuggester, which provides a list of books that the user would not like, or opposites of the book under consideration.

The **Zeitgeist** provides a snapshot of what is popular within a Web site community at any given time. LibraryThing has an extensive zeitgeist that includes top authors, top books, most reviewed books, highest rated, top tags, etc.

▶ FIGURE 7-4: LibraryThing: Zeitgeist

HOW ARE LIBRARIES USING SOCIAL CATALOGING?

Libraries are making use of social cataloging applications as tools for cataloging new titles in a browsable, interactive, user-focused community. They are utilizing these Web sites as a collection development tool and benefiting from the massive amount of reader recommendations therein, such as the 180,000 reviews on LibraryThing. They are integrating tools like widgets in order to easily display book covers to patrons on their Web sites and blogs. Libraries today are reaching out to where their users are and, by establishing a presence within these communities, are providing a portal to their library Web site and full OPAC.

The Washington State Library's New Books

http://wastatelib.wordpress.com

The newest books acquired by the Washington State Library are featured on the front page of their public blog via a LibraryThing widget. While creating a blog to promote the library and its services, Librarian Mary Schaff created a complementary library catalog of over 200 new titles on the social cataloging Web site LibraryThing. Random titles from that online catalog are fed in through RSS feeds and displayed within the sidebar of the library blog. Patrons are able to subscribe to the recent books' RSS feed or click in to browse the library's social catalog.

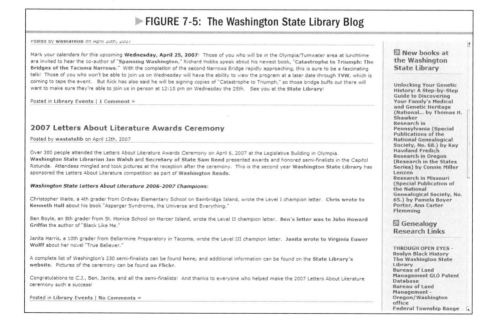

▶ FIGURE 7-5: The Washington State Library Blog

The project was conceived as both a means to introduce patrons to the library's collection and to work around the limitations of their traditional library catalog. "We needed a way to push our library's content out into the world and then pull new patrons into our collection, who would never have discovered us otherwise," said Schaff.

Schaff chose to implement a Web 2.0 catalog because of the usability and social functionality intrinsic to these applications, such as tagging, RSS feeds, and user profiles. The LibraryThing program was attractive because of its rich feature development and affordability. "They are constantly adding new features, so while new book cataloging sites are emerging, LibraryThing stays ahead of the pack," Schaff reported.

The library has promoted its new book feature, as well as its new blog, through handouts at library events, by issuing a press release, and through a prominent Flash display on their main library Web site. Although the project is only a few months old, Schaff has observed a consistent click-through rate from the new books display to their LibraryThing account, as well as a new source of traffic from their social catalog profile on LibraryThing, back to the blog.

Schaff found that when she initially began tagging books within LibraryThing, she was using library terminology, such as "reference," to describe books. She is now changing those tags to subject-oriented descriptors that will hold more meaning for patrons.

Schaff is highly satisfied with the LibraryThing application, although she hopes that they make their new graphical widget more user-friendly for non-techies. She would recommend the program to other libraries who wish to complement their existing catalogs. "LibraryThing has the ability to push content at the user, unlike a standard catalog that must wait for a user to come, and then figure out how to search it," Schaff concluded. (Mary Schaff, e-mail correspondence with author, February–March 2007)

The Danbury Library and LibraryThing for Libraries

www.danburylibrary.org

The Danbury Library has transformed their OPAC into a Library 2.0 experience for their patrons and is leading the way in library innovation as the first to integrate the LibraryThing for Libraries service into its online catalog. This new technology draws on the social functionality found in the LibraryThing application and offers user tags, ratings and reviews, book recommendations, and other edition information. The Danbury Library has chosen to implement the tagged browsing feature that provides user-created tags for each book in the catalog. Library patrons can browse the Danbury collection by clicking on these keywords in order to view other resources similarly classified by LibraryThing users. They also offer the recommendation functionality, which suggests similar

---

▶ **FIGURE 7-6: The Danbury (CT) Library**

Author	Tolkien, J. R. R. (John Ronald Reuel), 1892-1973
Title	The fellowship of the ring : being the first part of The lord of the rings / by J.R.R. Tolkien
Publisher	Boston : Houghton Mifflin Co., c1993

LOCATION	CALL #	STATUS
Main floor books	FIC TOLKIEN v.1	DUE 06-22-07
Main floor books	FIC TOLKIEN v.1	CHECK SHELVES
2nd Floor Young Adults	YAFIC TOLKIEN, pt.1	CHECK SHELVES
2nd Floor Young Adults	YAFIC TOLKIEN, pt.1	CHECK SHELVES

Edition	2nd ed
Descript	viii, 423 p., [1] folded leaf of plates : ill. (some col.) ; 23 cm
Series	The lord of the rings / by J.R.R. Tolkien ; pt 1
	Lord of the rings ; pt. 1
Note	"Note on the text" / David A. Anderson: p. [v]-viii
Subject	Baggins, Frodo (Fictitious character) -- Fiction
	Middle Earth (Imaginary place) -- Fiction
	Fantasy
ISBN	0395489318
Other editions and translations	The fellowship of the ring : being the first part of The lord of the rings by Tolkien, J. R. R. (John Ronald Reuel) (ISBN 0786251786)
	The fellowship of the ring [book on discs] by Tolkien, J. R. R. (John Ronald Reuel) (ISBN 0788739573)
	El Señor de los Anillos by Tolkien, J. R. R. (John Ronald Reuel) (ISBN 8445071408)
	El Señor de los Anillos by Tolkien, J. R. R. (John Ronald Reuel) (ISBN 8445071769)
	El Señor de los Anillos by Tolkien, J. R. R. (John Ronald Reuel) (ISBN 8445071777)
Similar Books	The two towers : being the second part of The Lord of the Rings by Tolkien, J. R. R. (John Ronald Reuel)
	The return of the king : being the third part of The lord of the rings by Tolkien, J. R. R. (John Ronald Reuel)
	The voyage of the Dawn Treader by Lewis, C. S. (Clive Staples)
	The silver chair by Lewis, C. S. (Clive Staples)
	Master of Middle-earth: the fiction of J. R. R. Tolkien [by] Paul H. Kocher by Kocher, Paul Harold
Tags	adventure british classics elves epic epic fantasy **fantasy** hobbits literature lord of the rings magic middle earth **tolkien**

---

titles to readers for each book in the collection. Finally, Danbury is utilizing the other editions service, which displays translations and alternate editions of titles owned by the library. By implementing this service, the Danbury Library not only has channeled additional functionality for its library patrons, but incorporated a massive resource of focused user-generated content. This customizable service enabled them to enhance their user experience while maintaining the previous functionality of their OPAC, as well as to remain within their brand environment.

Other Ways Libraries Are Using Social Cataloging

New Acquisitions

The Shenandoah (IA) Public Library catalogs their new books in LibraryThing and displays the new acquisitions on their library's Web site at: www.shenandoah.lib.ia.us and the Anita Public Library feeds in new books from their LibraryThing collection on their home page at: www.anita.swilsa.lib.ia.us

Web Site Gadgets

The Carl A. Pescosolido Library at The Governor's Academy in Byfield, features random books from their LibraryThing shelf on their blog at: http://thepesky library.blogspot.com, while Creston, Iowa's Gibson Memorial Library utilizes the LibraryThing widget tool to display recently acquired titles on the front page of their Web site at: www.creston.lib.ia.us. The Learning Resource Center Web site at Southwestern Community College (IA) links to their LibraryThing catalog, which displays items from their collection at: www.swcciowa.edu/LRC/LRC.html

Subject-Specific Collections

The Schulz Library at the Center for Cartoon Studies (White River Junction, VT) keeps its catalog of over 3,200 titles related to graphic novels on LibraryThing at: www.librarything.com/profile/CartoonStudies, while the Southwest Iowa Library Service Area supports local libraries and uses LibraryThing to present books from their professional collection on their resources page at: www.swilsa.lib.ia.us/collections.htm. The Research Institute on Addictions (RIA) Library of Buffalo, New York, keeps its collection of nearly 1,000 items related to the disease of addiction on LibraryThing at: www.librarything.com/profile/RIAlibrary

Display Cover Art

The Teen Corner of the Franklin Township (NJ) Public Library Web site exhibits cover art for titles recommended by the Young Adult Librarian from their Library-Thing catalog at: www.franklintwp.org/teenmainpage.htm, and the Atlantic (IA) Public Library catalogs their new titles in LibraryThing in order to present new book covers on their Web site at: www.atlantic.lib.ia.us

Social OPAC

The Ann Arbor (MI) District Library has incorporated custom-developed social features into their online catalog, such as tagging, book recommendations, ratings, and patron reviews, at: www.aadl.org/catalog, while the Hennepin County (MN) Library allows their patrons to comment on catalog items and create reader book lists at: www.hclib.org/pub/bookspace

HOW ARE LIBRARIANS USING SOCIAL CATALOGING?

Librarians are very active within social cataloging communities. They are cataloging their personal collections, as well as those of their libraries. They are seeking book recommendations, writing reviews, forming groups, rating books, and participating in new book talks.

Librarians Who LibraryThing

The leading social cataloging Web site, LibraryThing, allows members to form groups that serve as virtual neighborhoods within the larger community structure. Nearly 2,100 members belong to the "Librarians Who LibraryThing" group within the social networking environment. Librarians who are members are able to view and browse the catalogs of other members and discover which books are most commonly shared amongst the group's 650,000 books cataloged. Members post to the group's message board to give and receive advice about cataloging, developing taxonomies, tagging, and other professional topics. Librarians can subscribe via RSS to receive updates about new messages, new books added, and even new members.

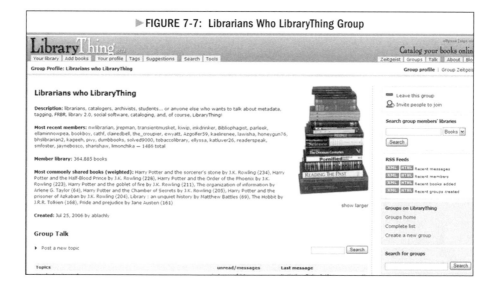

▶ FIGURE 7-7: Librarians Who LibraryThing Group

SOCIAL CATALOGING APPLICATIONS

LibraryThing

www.librarything.com

Available in multiple languages, LibraryThing is the clear leader in this space, with 250,000 members and 17 million books cataloged. The popular book-cataloging Web site is a partner of AbeBooks, which owns 40 percent of it. Members can both import and export their catalogs with LibraryThing, and it offers users access to their catalogs through mobile devices, as well as RSS feeds for tags, members, groups, and message boards.

Shelfari

www.shelfari.com

Similar to LibraryThing, Shelfari is a social cataloging Web site for books. Amazon.com is a major investor in the Shelfari Web site. Apart from providing members with the standard features of these applications, Shelfari provides Dewey call numbers with cataloging records, along with areas for user notes about the book, such as purchase date, condition, and signed information. Shelfari is one of the few cataloging Web sites that permits members to place their books on loan and record the loan and due dates, as well as the borrower's name.

Listal

www.listal.com

Listal is a cataloging application for more than just books. Members can keep track of their collections of books, movies, TV shows, video games, DVDs, and music on this Web site. Listal members can import and export their catalogs, create favorites lists, browse members by interest areas, and can comment on and rate not only titles, but actors, artists, authors, and directors. Members can place items on loan and compare the similarity of their interests with friends utilizing a tool that displays similarity percentages according to media type.

Gurulib

www.gurulib.com

Gurulib lets members catalog libraries of books, music, movies, games, and software. Less social than other applications of this kind, Gurulib allows members to designate their collections private or public. Members can add multiple shelves of books, import and export their catalogs, create wishlists, subscribe to members via RSS feeds, and set up price watchlists for items.

Squirl

http://squirl.info

For the collector at heart, there is Squirl, a cataloging system for records, movies, books, comic books, stamps, coins, and just about anything else. Members of Squirl can effectively set up any and all types of collections, from miniature cups and saucers, to action figures, to vintage scrimshaw. Users may set up unlimited collections and make some of them public and others private. Squirl members can form groups and subscribe to comments, collections, and forum messages via RSS feeds.

SOCIAL LISTS

In addition to social cataloging programs, there are a slew of Web sites available for people to create lists to share, instead of cataloging records. Today's users are creating lists of items they are using, items they want, and goals they want to achieve, and are sharing them with others in the community.

AllConsuming

http://allconsuming.net

AllConsuming is a Web site that allows members to list the objects they are currently consuming, including books, albums, movies, and food, and then rate and comment on them once they have been consumed. Members can ask the community for recommendations, view what is popular, and subscribe to RSS feeds.

43Things

www.43things.com

Life goal list maker 43Things provides a place where members can create lists of their aspirations and share them with others. Members can cheer each other on, work in groups to achieve a goal, discuss objectives, and find out how many people who have accomplished it think it was worthwhile.

Kaboodle

www.kaboodle.com

Kaboodle is a wishlist Web site. Members can create multiple public or private wishlists of items they covet from anywhere on the Web. Hyperlinked items are listed with photos, price information, and member notes and can be reserved for purchase by other members, serving as a cyber gift registry. Reservations are hidden from the member who can rate desired items according to priority. Kaboodle was acquired by the Hearst Corporation in August 2007.

BEST PRACTICES

▶ **Tag for Readers**. Think about the ways in which your library patrons would describe the books in your collection and then use their language to tag book entries. Your goal is to make items findable by your patrons, so consider their perspective as you assign keywords.

▶ **Provide Subscription Options**. Many social cataloging Web sites offer the ability to subscribe to users' collections of books and media via RSS feeds. If you are using one such application, be sure and let your patrons know that by subscribing they can be automatically updated when you add new books to your virtual shelf, or even when you write new reviews.

▶ **Include the Full Name of Your Library**. Oftentimes libraries and organizations choose an acronym as their user name in social cataloging communities, so it is important to be sure to provide the full name of your library in a place that is highly visible within your profile.

▶ **Write Reviews**. This is the perfect environment for librarians to post book reviews and make recommendations for their patrons, as well as the entire community. Your patrons can subscribe to your review feed and receive notifications each time you post a new review; what better way to keep the library fresh in people's minds?

▶ **Make the Most of the Community**. Let selectors know about these communities so that they can gauge the popularity of titles in their subject fields. Inform reference staff about these robust environments which provide free book review collections.

▶ **Catalog Books You Have Authored**. Librarians should be sure to add books that they or their peers have authored to their virtual shelf, since these communities can serve as good marketing outlets. Also, ask colleagues to write reviews.

▶8

VIDEO SHARING

The user-generated movement of the new Web has sparked a video revolution in which everyday users can make movies and become famous. Through online video-sharing communities, "average Joes" are able to upload and share their home movies with the world. In today's new Internet order, we are witnessing the evolution of the audience; a progression from observer to director, which places the user in charge of what, how, and when they consume content, and anticipates a culture of creators who invent their own entertainment.

Online video-sharing Web sites such as YouTube, Metacafe, and Revver enable millions of people to share, rate, comment on, tag, watch, and gather around video content free of charge and technical expertise. Creators are able to upload their videos without worrying about the proper file format, as these applications automatically convert their clips for them. Viewers are able to watch videos without having to download and install any special software, as players are embedded within the Web sites.

Amateur filmmakers, video diarists, karaoke hopefuls, and talented pets have all been given a forum to display their work through this DIY entertainment model. People are online watching vacation videos, sitcoms shot on a shoestring, and home-brewed talk shows within communities where they can be discussed and reviewed.

Major corporations such as Coca-Cola, Dove, and IBM have discovered online video to be a powerful marketing medium and have begun broadcasting their personalities and building their brands through low-cost streaming ad campaigns. Businesses like Enterprise Rent-a-Car and Google are giving potential employees a behind-the-scenes peek at their corporate culture in their recruitment videos, while other companies, such as Deloitte, are creating short films for professional development training. Yale University has made video lectures for seven of their 2007 courses freely available online, inviting people to share in the Ivy League experience. And the White House has taken its war on drugs to the Web, posting several of its public services messages to YouTube.

In 2006, over 79 percent of broadband Web users watched online videos, and it has been predicted by eMarketer that this video-viewing population will reach legion proportions at 157 million by the year 2010 (Holahan, 2007: 2). Online video is the new direction of media exchange on the Web, as evidenced by the $1.65 billion Google purchase of YouTube, the Net's fourth most-popular user destination.

Today's users are embracing the authentic handiwork of their peers over the spoon-fed programming provided by major media outlets and are redefining current archetypes of entertainment. Members of video-sharing Web sites are forming communities around shared content and experiences while sustaining a vehicle that empowers themselves and their neighbors to achieve stardom. Today's users are fast-forwarding to a new chapter in the culture of the Web.

INSIDE VIDEO SHARING

As with many Web 2.0 applications, video-sharing Web sites tempt people with a variety of unique features and services. Some up-and-coming startups are even offering their members monetary rewards for quality content. There are, however, some basic features that are customary to most of these new Web programs. This chapter takes a look at these through the industry leader, YouTube, which is home to 60 percent of all videos watched on the Web.

▶ FIGURE 8-1: Inside Video Sharing: YouTube Home Page

The **Top Videos** of the moment are featured on nearly all video-sharing Web sites. By spotlighting the top-rated, most "favorited," and most discussed video clips, these applications enable members to browse by the most popular clips within the community. The main form of navigation on media-sharing Web sites is browsing, which engenders discovery. On sites such as YouTube, members can also browse by category, channel, or community group.

Ratings based on a five-star grading system may be assigned to video clips by members. These scores are tallied and offered to the community as a gauge of video quality.

Channel Pages are user profiles that aggregate all of a member's videos in one place, creating an excellent tool for businesses and organizations who wish to establish a brand presence in these communities. Channels allow members to view the video collections of other users, as well as to subscribe to receive new content updates.

Tags, or descriptive keywords, may be attached to videos by content creators, just as in photo-sharing applications, in order to make them more findable. An additional feature offered by some video-sharing Web sites includes the ability for authors to "deep-tag," or to assign tags to designated scenes within the video itself. This functionality makes clips more searchable and also allows the viewer to jump

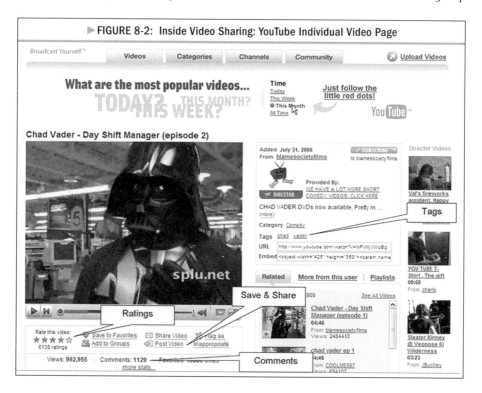

▶ FIGURE 8-2: Inside Video Sharing: YouTube Individual Video Page

to a particular scene, catering to the on-demand preferences of today's Web user. Instead of watching a five-minute video of Golden Globes highlights, members could skip to the 30-second acceptance speech of their favorite winner.

Save and Share options are available within all video-sharing communities. They permit the user to save videos to favorites lists, create playlists, share with friends via e-mail or IM, add to other social sites such as del.icio.us, or post the clip to their blog. These community tools that allow members to connect with others are key to the video-sharing environments where popularity is dependant upon word-of-mouth endorsements.

Comments can be made on video clips just as on blog posts, photos, and other shared media on new Web 2.0 sites. Videos on popular Web sites such as YouTube can receive comments from thousands of viewers who ignite and participate in conversations with their peers.

HOW ARE LIBRARIES USING VIDEO SHARING?

Libraries are tapping into the power of video as a way to promote library programs and services, provide library instruction, and engage the community. They are creating library tours, staff videos, reading program commercials, and guides to library collections. Libraries have begun to create profile, or channel, pages in major video-sharing communities and are reaching out to users through this new medium.

Arlington Heights Memorial Library LibVlog

www.ahml.info

http://tinyurl.com/25nkjn

The Arlington Heights (IL) Memorial Library produces a popular video Weblog, called LibVlog, which is funded by a grant from the federal Library Services and Technology Act (LSTA). They film a weekly "What's Up at the Library" series, hosted by library staffers Jenny and Mike who highlight library services, upcoming events, and occasionally offer a behind-the-scenes look at the inner workings of the library. This regular Monday episode is introduced by local business leaders and community members who are invited to make guest appearances. Additional library videos include author talks and snippets from library programs such as: a Harry Potter book discussion group, highlights from a library book sale, cooking tips classes with Chef David Esau, and Manga drawing techniques sessions. The library films two to three video segments each week ranging in length between two and five minutes.

In an effort to add a more personal dimension to the library as well as to inform patrons about upcoming events, Library Web Services Manager Ingrid Lebolt joined with Executive Producer Josh Pfluger to helm the LibVlog project in fall

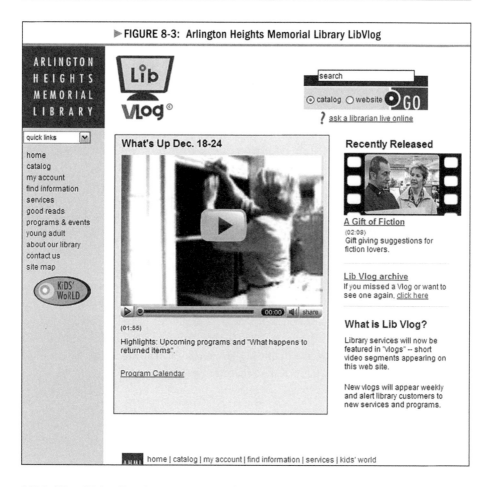

▶ FIGURE 8-3: Arlington Heights Memorial Library LibVlog

2006. "Our Web effort is attempting to bring everything possible to the library user via the computer—a virtual branch, if you will," remarked Lebolt.

The team decided to utilize video technology and to have it hosted on YouTube. The library is able to embed these YouTube files within their own library Web site without having to store the videos themselves. Many of the vlog episodes are produced by the professional Library Production Studios; however, the library also contributes with their own amateur equipment. The team uses Camtasia, a capture program for recording actions on a computer screen, and the MacIntosh video-editing programs iMovie '06 and Final Cut Pro 5.1 for post-production. All of their videos are output into Quicktime format for easy uploading to YouTube.

The library marketed their vlog through e-mail campaigns, a series of newspaper ads, and word-of-mouth within the community. They are planning a bookmobile banner as their next promotional device. The library has seen a growth in program participation since the launch of the LibVlog, as well as a sense of enthusiasm amongst library staff and the community as a whole. AHML was recognized with a national InfoTubey Award in April 2007, which was presented to the top five library video productions that enhanced the value of their libraries and demonstrated creativity and humor in library marketing.

Lebolt advises other libraries who are considering a project like this one to set manageable goals and consider allocating time for each piece of the production, such as: script-writing, scene planning, finding locations, gathering props, shooting background footage, filming the clip, and post-production work. (Ingrid Lebolt, e-mail correspondence with author, March 2007)

Other Ways Libraries Are Using Video Sharing

Marketing and Promotion

The teen readers at the Public Library of Charlotte and Mecklenburg County (NC) helped create a summer reading program commercial, highlighting prizes and program rules at: http://tinyurl.com/37coxe, while the Lexington (KY) Public Library is using video for outreach to their community through their library card commercials at: http://tinyurl.com/2q6vrw. Through engaging videos and characters, such as the Super Librarian, the McCracken County (KY) Library promotes upcoming events and programs including Dr. Duck's Storytime, a Star Wars weekend, and live homework help at: http://tinyurl.com/36yyju

Library Staff

The St. Joseph County (IN) Public Library has created a behind-the-scenes look at their library by filming a day in the life of their library staff at: http://tinyurl.com/2gauex

Library Tours

The Park Library of Springfield, Ohio, has created a video tour of their branch library at: http://tinyurl.com/39jm7x, and the Reference Librarians at the Williams College (MA) Library have created a Library Mystery Tour welcoming new students at: http://tinyurl.com/36k6g9. The Elmwood Park (IL) Public Library celebrates 70 years with this library tour at: http://tinyurl.com/329ycy

Library Events

The Clark County (OH) Public Library has created a YouTube channel featuring videos from all of their branch libraries, including clips of library events such as teen Dance Revolution night, Discovery Saturday, and a Pajama Party, at: http://tinyurl. com/2rtjb4; the Hartford County (CT) Public Library celebrates its 60-year anniversary in their videos at: http://tinyurl.com/2oj5hp. The Denver Public Library challenged their teen patrons to create fun library videos in their YouTube video contest, which was featured on their MySpace page at: http://myspace.com/denver_evolver

Staff Training

The Allen County (IN) Public Library has created videos informing staff about new wireless connectivity in the library, as well as training for using a new phone system, at: http://tinyurl.com/2a432v

Library Instruction

The library at the Georgia Institute of Technology provides students with Webcasts instructing them how to conduct cited reference searches, find journals, use electronic resources, and conduct patent searches at: http://tinyurl.com/2uh6t8, while the Tampa Bay Library Consortium has created public service videos featuring library services such as Ask a Librarian, online borrowing, and Web access, and encourages other libraries to download, personalize, and use them for their own library promotion at: http://tinyurl.com/2v9odd

Library Resources

The librarians and staff at the Gail Borden Library (Elgin, IL) recommend books for youth and adult readers in their videos at: http://tinyurl.com/2wrqen, and the Fulton County (IN) Public Library features library resources in their commercial at: http://tinyurl.com/2ssgg2. The Kenton (KY) Public Library talks about genealogy, local history, and quilting in its video blog series "Off the Shelf," which is available through iTunes and their library Web site at: www.kentonlibrary.org/media/offtheshelf/index.cfm

HOW ARE LIBRARIANS USING VIDEO SHARING?

Librarians are joining video-sharing communities such as YouTube and blip.tv to explore user-created films, as well as to share their own videos with the world. They are joining and forming groups, rating and commenting on video clips, and keeping up with today's users.

Library Conferences and Event Videos

Librarians are offering peers and interested viewers a glimpse into library conferences and events by posting their own video footage of the professional happenings. Librarians not in attendance at the American Library Association 2006 annual conference can share in the experience by watching the Bookcart Drill Team Competition and the ACRL Information Literacy Pom-Pom Squad. Those unable to travel to TechExpress 2006 can view clips of talks given by Michael Stephens, Jenny Levine, and Stephen Abram. And those not present at Internet

▶ FIGURE 8-4: Library Event Videos

Librarian 2006 can see a portion of Elizabeth Lane Lawley's closing keynote address, or watch scenes from the local Monterey Bay area. These videos provide a window into remote events, making them accessible to a global community.

VIDEO-SHARING APPLICATIONS

In the realm of online video, there are two basic market sectors to recognize: streaming and downloadable video. Streaming video is played back completely within a browser and is not saved or downloaded onto the user's computer. Often the format used to distribute short video clips, streaming video technology is utilized by YouTube and other video-sharing Web sites. Downloadable video consists of files that can be downloaded for permanent or semi-permanent use on a user's computer. The method of choice for full-length features, pay-per downloadable video files can be found through sellers such as Amazon and iTunes.

YouTube

www.youtube.com

Owned by Google, YouTube is the clear market leader, with over 34 million unique users per month (Thaw, 2006). Each day, YouTube streams more than 100 million video clips and sees over 65,000 more uploaded.

Yahoo! Video

http://video.yahoo.com

Yahoo! Video shares the same feature set as YouTube. Members are allowed to upload, rate, and review video clips, establish channel pages, tag videos, and browse by category or most popular. In addition, a Yahoo! Video search yields results from across the Web.

Metacafe

www.metacafe.com

This independent Israeli startup boasts over 1 million unique users daily and streams over 400 million video clips per month. Aside from the basic features, Metacafe offers its members a rewards program that enables them to earn cash for popular movies.

Revver

http://one.revver.com/revver

Revver is a video-sharing service that attaches ads to members' video clips and then utilizes a unique technology that tracks video views across the Internet. Revver shares the ad revenue resulting from those views with video creators. From inside Revver, users can share their videos with a number of community sites, build a widget to share video collections on a Web site or blog, and opt into mobile distribution.

Motionbox

www.motionbox.com

Motionbox is a video-sharing community with some unique features. Most significantly, Motionbox allows creators to deep-tag their videos, or tag specific sections within their clips. Viewers can then jump to a specific tag within the video rather than watching the whole thing. Designed with personal video in mind, Motionbox allows members to keep their video clips private or share them only among family and friends. Members can select and share segments from within a video clip and can scroll through and preview entire video clips from within thumbnail views.

BEST PRACTICES

▶ **Use a Popular Video Host**. Be sure to upload your video to one of the major video-hosting services, such as YouTube or Metacafe, which will offer you maximum exposure to your audience. These hosting services are free and will enable you to embed your videos into your own Web pages as if you were hosting them yourself.

▶ **Utilize Free Editing Tools**. Editing a short video clip should not necessitate expensive editing tools. You should be able to achieve your goals with applications that come installed with most computers today, such as Windows Movie Maker or iMovie. Alternatively, you can seek out free Web 2.0 video editing tools, such as Jumpcut or Eyespot.

▶ **Keep It Short**. Remember that this format consists of short video clips, not full-feature films. The majority of the all-time top-rated videos on YouTube clock in at under six minutes, and a good number of them range between two and three.

▶ **Create a Brand Channel**. Nearly all of these video-sharing Web sites offer the ability to create a channel page that is similar to a user profile and includes all videos by an individual or organization. Some of these channels allow custom wallpaper or background images, a company logo, and contact information. A channel page such as this could be an additional outreach tool and serve as another portal to your organization and your Web site.

▶ **Storyboard Your Videos**. Approach your library video like you would any other movie you were creating. Take time in the pre-production phase to brainstorm about the scenes you would like to include, the story you would like to tell, and then map out those images in the form of storyboards.

▶ **Write a Script**. You might be creating a video that is tightly scripted, with a definite list of points to cover, or you may want participants to improvise and just have fun. But even if you want your video to be spontaneous, you will want to consider creating a bare-bones script for yourself and others to refer to. Include key concepts that you want each actor to convey during the film in order to provide them with a jumping-off point for each scene.

▶ **Have a Goal**. Before you begin your video project, you will want to think about what it is you want to achieve with your video. What will be the goal of your film? Will it be a marketing film that will aim to spotlight user services and programs, or an instructional video meant to teach?

REFERENCES

Holahan, Catherine. "Long Live the Net Video Revolution." *Business Week* (January 2, 2007). Available: www.businessweek.com/technology/content/jan2007/tc20070102_878225. htm (accessed January 20, 2007).

Thaw, Jonathan. "Google Reportedly in Talks to Buy YouTube for $1.6b." *The Boston Globe* (October 7, 2006). Available: www.boston.com/business/personaltech/articles/ 2006/10/07/google_reportedly_in_talks_to_buy_youtube_for_16b/ (accessed November 5, 2006).

▶9

PERSONALIZED START PAGES

eir to the 1990s' customizable portal, a new breed of personalized start page has emerged—a variety that enables users to aggregate a wealth of information on a single page with the ease of drag-and-drop functionality. Owing to the proliferation of RSS and the development of AJAX technology, these Web 1.0 descendants offer users much more than daily horoscopes and local weather, and are the means by which most people unsuspectingly utilize RSS technology.

Web 2.0 start pages allow users to gather content from anywhere on the Internet in an online space. Users can collect and display their favorite news sources, blog feeds, Flickr photos, Google Docs, del.icio.us bookmarks, MySpace profiles, Netflix queues, personal calendars, and e-mail accounts all in one place, and can access this collection from any computer with an Internet connection. Users have the ability to add virtually any data with an RSS feed to their page, as well as create new content on the fly, such as to-do lists and sticky notes. These portable home-pages make use of widgets that display information within modular customizable boxes.

Web portals such as Google, Yahoo!, and Microsoft are each offering their users such organizational spaces, while at the same time furnishing a gateway to their other Web properties. Over 60 million users aggregate their personalized content through a MyYahoo! start page, but small independent startups such as Netvibes and Pageflakes, which are offering brand-neutral services, are becoming strong contenders. They have won over millions of users by providing members with a choice of thousands of widgets ranging from chat boxes to Sudoku puzzles, many of which were created by other Web users.

Major media franchises such as ESPN, *The New York Times*, and *The Wall Street Journal* have noted this growing trend and begun offering their users exclusive content, such as videos, programming, and sports scores, in hopes that they will customize their browsing experience through their own start pages.

Through personalized start pages, users have the ability to organize, manage, and customize their data and information in a centralized and portable location. People no longer need to navigate to multiple Web sites to gather their preferred news, events, television listings, Web searches, daily schedules, eBay auctions, and stock quotes, but merely have to sign in to their own private portal.

START PAGE FEATURES

There are many varieties of personalized start pages, each offering its own set of widgets, interface display, and functionality; however, there is a set of core features common to all of these applications.

Widgets, also called gadgets, modules, and flakes by different start page applications, consist of lightweight application boxes that display Web content, often through an RSS feed. They can consume content ranging from blog feeds and eBay auctions to bookmark lists and daily calendars.

Multiple **Tabs** or pages can be created by the user in order to separate start page content into categories or sections, such as work vs. personal. Some of these applications provide templates for tabs pre-populated with widgets relevant to topics such as shopping, finance, and business.

The **Add Content** section, available within every start page application, allows users to pick and choose which gadgets they want to include on their pages. Content types include news feeds, podcasts, and mini-application modules such as weather or e-mail display boxes.

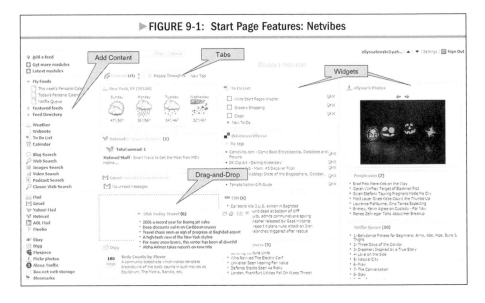

▶ FIGURE 9-1: Start Page Features: Netvibes

Drag-and-Drop functionality allows users to organize their start pages by simply dragging widgets to a preferred place on the page and dropping them in. This makes organization quick and easy for the user who can shuffle and reorganize information according to changing priorities or preferences.

START PAGE POTENTIAL IN LIBRARIES

Librarians and information professionals create and access a large amount of information on a daily basis. They consume news, bookmark Web pages, create calendar appointments, conduct database searches, upload photos and video files, read e-mail, and scan scores and headlines. Personalized start pages are a time-conscious tool for managing a surplus of dispersed Web content.

Arizona State University Start Pages

Arizona State University has partnered with Google to provide personalized start pages to their academic community. Utilizing Google's customizable start page service, which is part of their Apps for Education software suite, the university is able to offer a branded experience from within the school's domain while benefiting from Google's infrastructure. Students may customize their start pages with Google and third-party compatible widgets alongside fixed content that has been pre-determined by the school. ASU can provide students and faculty with campus

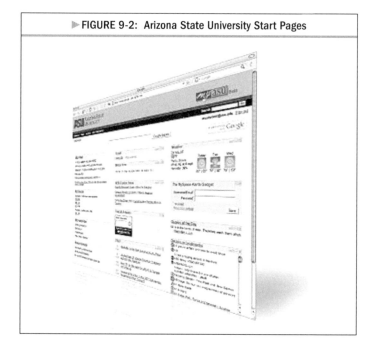

▶ FIGURE 9-2: Arizona State University Start Pages

news, announcements, course information, and interactive services, along with Google services such as e-mail, IM, calendars, and search.

Other Ways Libraries Can Use Start Pages

Subject Guides

Libraries could create start pages that serve as tabbed subject guides for patrons, leading to research-related online resources according to topic.

Library Portals

Start pages could be used as a public aggregation portal for libraries, gathering all of their distributed online content in one place for patrons to access, such as: podcasts, blog postings, Flickr photos, YouTube videos, recommended del.icio.us links, LibraryThing bookshelf, and Google map directions.

Organizational Tools

Start pages can be an invaluable organizational tool for information professionals to manage all of their news feeds, research sources, and productivity tools, and subject specialists could benefit from utilizing start pages to organize research resources.

Collaboration

Start pages could be shared or made public in order to collaborate among libraries or fellow librarians, or staffers within one library.

Intranet Tools

Start page services, such as Google Apps for Business, can be branded for use within the enterprise. Libraries could use them to provide their organization with a branded start page for employees.

START PAGE APPLICATIONS

Netvibes
www.netvibes.com

Netvibes offers users over 100,000 widgets, including podcasts, tab templates, news feeds, and modules. The service is available in 50 languages, including Norwegian, Corsican, and Turkish, and can even be accessed through the Nintendo Wii game system. Netvibes allows users to share their start page tabs with other users. Additionally, they offer branded "Universe" pages that display news feeds from leading content publishers.

Pageflakes
www.pageflakes.com

Pageflakes allows members to share their pages with other users or make them accessible to the public as community portals through their Pagecasting feature. It provides over 230,000 widgets, some of which include an address book, calendar, del.icio.us links, Flickr photos, and YouTube videos.

Google Start Page
www.google.com/ig

Google's entry into this space is available for individuals, as well as for small to medium-sized businesses and educational organizations. Through its Google Apps for Your Domain project, it provides businesses and organizational institutes with the ability to customize and offer branded start pages to their users.

Windows Live
www.live.com

Windows Live.com is a Microsoft offering that provides a development space to create gadgets and allows users to import Online Processor Markup Language (OPML) files. They offer users hundreds of widgets and news feeds, as well as customizable display settings.

MyYahoo!
http://my.yahoo.com

MyYahoo! is the most widely used personalized start page on the market with over 60 million users. This personal portal allows users to add Yahoo! services to their pages, such as e-mail, stock portfolios, weather, and TV listings, along with hundreds of other widgets, feeds, and multimedia selections.

BEST PRACTICES

▶ **Add Your Own Content**. If you are setting up a start page for your library, be sure to add all of your own content and profiles to your library start page, such as your Flickr photos, del.icio.us bookmarks, online events calendar, YouTube videos, links to your library Web site, blogs, MySpace and Facebook profiles, etc.

▶ **Build a Portal**. Start page applications such as Netvibes and Pageflakes have added the ability to make public start pages that can be used to represent a company or organization as a branded portal and marketing device. Major corporations and media outlets such as Forbes and Time Inc. have created these Universes (Netvibes) and Pagecasts (Pageflakes) for their content. Libraries may wish to consider following suit, as these pages are public and can be accessed by patrons from any online computer.

▶ **Skip the Aquarium**. When designing your library start page, focus on the important content your patrons will need access to, and let them add the extraneous modules to their personalized pages. Personality is important in these social applications, but so is an uncluttered workspace.

▶ **Organize by Tabs**. The majority of start pages enable users to create separate pages accessed by tabs for their content. Organize your resources by creating new tabs for distinct subjects or formats, i.e., videos, podcasts, blogs, etc.

▶10

SOCIAL NETWORKING SOFTWARE

Times have changed, and so has the Web. What was once considered an ancillary feature of Web sites has suddenly become the *raison d'être*. Community-based social networking Web sites capture the essence of the new Web by encouraging individuality in tandem with offering a sense of belonging within a larger group. The phenomenon of social networking taps into the passions of Web users, allowing them to express themselves creatively in a social environment. They offer a portal to information, knowledge, and people, where members can share content and establish relationships with others.

Social networking Web sites are places where people gather to interact and relate with other members. They are environments where users can seek out like-minded people and build connections with them. Social networking venues foster an atmosphere of sharing and communication, and motivate members to mentor, befriend, learn from, and inspire their peers. They provide the tools necessary for people to be creative and to generate original content in forms ranging from blogs and journals to photos, videos, and customized user profiles.

Today we are seeing Web users congregating around real-life events, romance, niche interests, and careers. Community members are swapping parenting advice on Maya's Mom; karaoke fanatics are singing their hearts out and being judged by peers on Singshot; Baby Boomers are shaping the silvering Web in the Eons ecosystem; and our furry friends are mingling on Dogster.

These collective destinations are so ubiquitous that a recent study showed that one out of every 20 Internet visits goes to a social networking Web site. The largest social nexus today, MySpace is the fifth highest-trafficked Web site on the Internet. Its 130 million users see 8 million newbies sign up monthly (Hof, 2006). Facebook, the academic social networking site launched in 2004, now boasts 19 million users belonging to over 47,000 networks. There is a general impression of an all-youth populace within these virtual hangouts; however, the demographic trend has skewed consistently toward older users with time. Although hip with the tween set,

MySpace sees a whopping 51 percent of its population falling into the 35-plus age range in the U.S. Similarly, roughly 40 percent of Facebook's members are over the 35-year milestone (Lipsman, 2006).

Marketing moguls have not missed a beat with regard to these social marvels. Corporations such as Disney and Burger King have learned that settings like MySpace, where word-of-mouth reigns, offer great potential as vehicles for social marketing, and have established a presence in this new medium. Web stalwarts Google and Microsoft have each made advertising deals with MySpace and Facebook respectively, and media giant News Corp carved its niche with the $580 million purchase of MySpace in 2005.

Today's Web users want to feel free to be themselves, but they also want to feel that there are others out there like them. They want to find those people and add them to their social networks. It is this need that is fulfilled by these community-based Web sites, and it is what has made them the fastest growing sites on the Internet.

FEATURES OF SOCIAL NETWORKING SOFTWARE

Community-based social networking Web sites vary greatly in their appearance and subject focus; however, they do share several common features:

User Profiles are the heart of the social networking Web site. They allow members to create an online identity and point of origin within a site. Community members can customize their user profile to create a personalized presence within the network representative of their personality, interests, and perspective. These detailed profiles lead to the member's content, such as a blog or journal entries, groups to which they belong, their network of friends, user comments, their photo and videos files, as well as personal information about interests such as favorite books, films, music, and heroes.

Groups are sub-communities within a social networking Web site. They are places where members can subdivide into narrowly focused interest areas to meet and discuss relevant topics. Belonging to groups is a way of further developing and expressing identity within an online community.

User Blogs or journals are a creative outlet that many social networks provide. They are a means by which members can express themselves within the community, along with other content creation outlets such as photos and videos. By blogging or journaling within a community rather than on an independent blog, members are guaranteed exposure to a wide audience. This may explain why MySpace is the second most popular blogging software used in the U.S. according to a study by Pew Internet & American Life (Lenhart and Fox, 2006).

Send Message is a feature present in all social networking hubs. Communication is a critical element in any social atmosphere, and virtual ones are no exception.

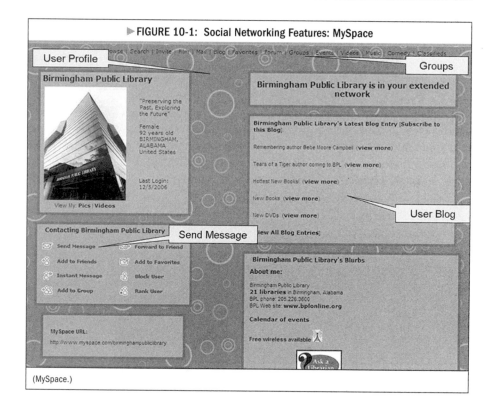

▷ FIGURE 10-1: Social Networking Features: MySpace

(MySpace.)

Online communities offer different options for communicating with other members, such as an internal e-mail messaging system, via personal e-mail, live chat, or through instant messaging.

Friends Lists are a feature provided by the vast majority of community Web sites today. They permit members to create a personal social network of friends, or connections within the community. Often the action of bestowing the "friend" status on another member denotes more than a social connection and can involve access or viewing rights to additional personal content. Some social networks offer advanced privacy features that enable members to establish permissions and restrictions for different sets of people within their network, including contacts, friends, and family.

User Comments enable members to engage in and ignite conversations within the community. They are a way for community members to interact with one another. On social networking sites, members are able to make comments on the content of others including: blog posts, videos, photos, news stories, and other users' profiles. Such comments can be considered a reflection of popularity and a form of social validation.

Browse Users enables members to navigate the community of members. Since the primary purpose of these social applications is to connect people to people,

▶ FIGURE 10-2: Social Networking Features: MySpace Friends List

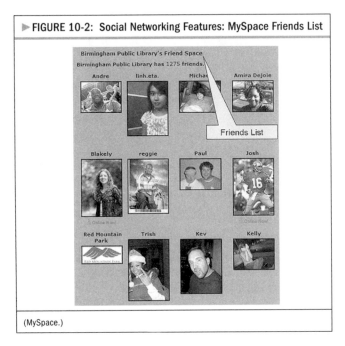

(MySpace.)

▶ FIGURE 10-3: Social Networking Features: MySpace Friends Comments

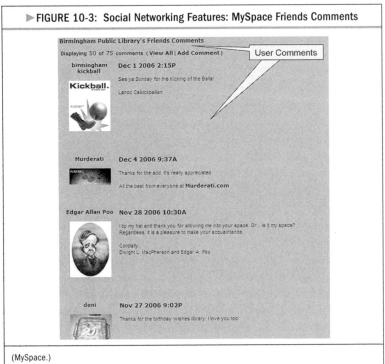

(MySpace.)

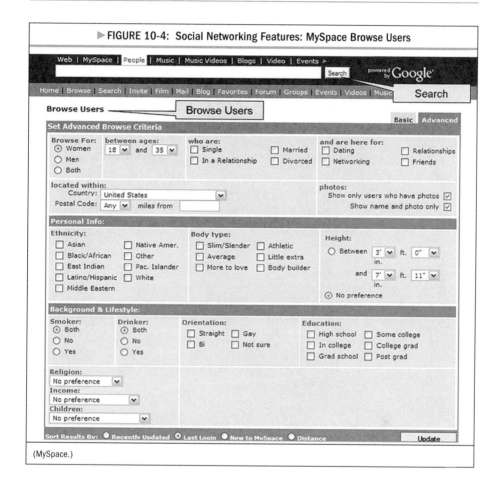

▷ FIGURE 10-4: Social Networking Features: MySpace Browse Users

(MySpace.)

they all provide a means of locating other users. Members are commonly able to browse by criteria, such as tag or keyword, but in some cases are offered detailed browse interfaces with advanced conditions.

Search is a feature found within all social networks. As quickly as members can browse to discover people, they can execute a keyword search to find them.

HOW ARE LIBRARIES USING SOCIAL NETWORKING?

Libraries are using social networking Web sites as vehicles for outreach and promotion, as portals to library Web sites, and as a means of connecting with patrons. Libraries are going where the users are by joining in these online communities. They are advertising and providing library services to patrons where they "live." The following successful examples highlight just a few of the more innovative uses of social networking by libraries.

▶ FIGURE 10-5: MyOwnCafe

MyOwnCafe

www.myowncafe.org

MyOwnCafe is an engaging online social networking community for teens in southeastern Massachusetts, who can sign in to find out about community events, regional sports, gaming news, and local jobs. Teens who join this massive library community can download .mp3 files from local bands; take quizzes and polls; chat in message boards about topics such as sports, anime, music, movies, poetry, and college advice; and, of course, utilize library resources. A grant-funded endeavor helmed by the Southeastern Massachusetts Library System (SEMLS), the MyOwnCafe Web site can be customized by any high school or public member library to offer their own electronic resources and databases and serve as their library's Web site.

Assistant Administrator for Technology Kathy Lussier teamed up with Vickie Been-Beavers, Assistant Administrator for Youth Services, to begin the project in the fall of 2004. "Libraries were struggling to develop and maintain their own Web sites . . . at the same time, we recognized there was the ever-present problem of keeping teens involved in the library," said Lussier. They were also eager to find a way to make access to library online resources easier.

The team put together a Teen Advisory Group (TAG), consisting of both librarians and teens, which provided the direction for the content and design of the Web site. Local teens took an active role in the development of MyOwnCafe, including supplying ideas for content, participating in the selection of the Web design team, choosing the final design, testing the beta Web site, and offering continual feedback about improvements. An outside Web design team was selected to create the Web site. They conducted surveys and held focus groups with teens before deciding on a final strategy.

The Web site developers decided to use a free open-source framework, called DotNetNuke, which allowed them to create a customizable community Web site compatible with their Windows 2003 server environment.

The librarians held informational sessions for youth services librarians in the SEMLS member libraries and demonstrated the Web site to library directors during membership meetings. SEMLS held a Web site kickoff party in February 2006 at a local mall and hired a band featured on MyOwnCafe to play during the event. They gave away gift cards, MyOwnCafe mugs, T-shirts, and pens to attending teens. They also held other promotional events, such as iPod Shuffle giveaways to teens who posted on the Web site.

The MyOwnCafe Web site has become a thriving teen community, with over 300 members aged 12–19 and over 11,000 posts to the message boards, which are moderated by teen leaders. Some of these online community bonds are translating into offline relationships, as teens sharing common interests are forming real-life groups such as the Anime Club, which meets regularly throughout the region.

Lussier recommends enabling people in such social networking environments to make live posts to a Web site rather than implementing an approval process. She advises that conversations happen rapidly online, and that any lag time in the appearance of posts would discourage the spontaneity of these discussions. They have found that letting the community mediate itself through teen moderators has worked very well. "Because it is their community, the teens are vigilant about making sure it is an interesting and enjoyable place to be," Lussier concluded.

Other Ways Libraries Are Using Social Networking

New Acquisitions

Within the MySpace community, the Birmingham (AL) Public Library blogs about new books, DVDs, and authors, providing patrons with links to the library's catalog and electronic databases for more information at: www.myspace.com/birmingham publiclibrary, and the Stoneham (MA) Public Library provides a slideshow of new book covers for patrons within their MySpace profile at: www.myspace.com/

stonehamlibrary. The Public Library of Charlotte and Mecklenburg County (NC) uses their MySpace profile to feature new book titles on their profile, which link back to their library catalog, at: www.myspace.com/libraryloft

Library Portals

The Brooklyn College (NY) Library profile in MySpace acts as a library portal with research links directing users to their Web site at: www.myspace.com/brooklyn collegelibrary, and the Young Adult Library Services Association (YALSA) division of the American Library Association (ALA) has a MySpace profile that links to their podcasts, del.icio.us links, Flickr photos, YALSA blog, and their main Web site at: www.myspace.com/yalsa. The ALA has a MySpace profile that displays their YouTube videos, Flickr photos, and incorporates a Meebo widget for live chat with the ALA at: www.myspace.com/atyourlibrary

Library Services Promotion

The University of Central Florida promotes their Ask a Librarian service through their user profile at: www.myspace.com/ucfaskalibrarian, while the Albany (NY) Public Library uses their MySpace profile to promote their Online Teen Book Club at: www.myspace.com/acplwy

Remote Library Catalog

The Hennepin County (MN) Library allows patrons to search the OPAC from a search box displayed on their MySpace profile at: www.myspace.com/hennepin countylibrary

Library Events

The Perry-Castaneda Library within the University of Texas at Austin uses their MySpace profile to display a detailed library workshop calendar at: www.myspace. com/utlibraries

Library News and Information

The University of Illinois at Urbana-Champaign Undergraduate Library blogs about study hours and library events at: http://myspace.com/undergradlibrary, and the library hours and contact information are displayed on the user profile of the Thomas Ford Memorial Library (Western Springs, IL) at: http://myspace. com/thomasford. The Westmont (IL) Public Library offers patrons their IM handles and other library information from their user profile at: http://myspace. com/westmontlibrary

Library Resources

The Morrisville (NY) College Libraries link to library reference resources, online databases, and their special collections from their MySpace user profile at:

www.myspace.com/morrisvillecollegelibrary, and the Warsaw (IN) Community Public Library features their library RSS feed on their MySpace page at: www. myspace.com/warsawlibrary

HOW ARE LIBRARIANS USING SOCIAL NETWORKING?

Librarians are utilizing social networking sites to participate in the social Web. They are joining in the global conversation that is happening within these ecosystems. Librarians are creating, consuming, organizing, and sharing knowledge and information within these online communities. They are forming connections and building social capital amongst their peers, library patrons, and Web users.

Facebook

www.facebook.com

Librarians are joining and creating user profiles within Facebook, the social networking community for colleges and universities. From within the community they are reaching out to students and faculty, to offer research assistance, IM services, and establish an online presence. Librarians on Facebook are blogging, posting photos, joining groups and networks, and sharing their experience and expertise.

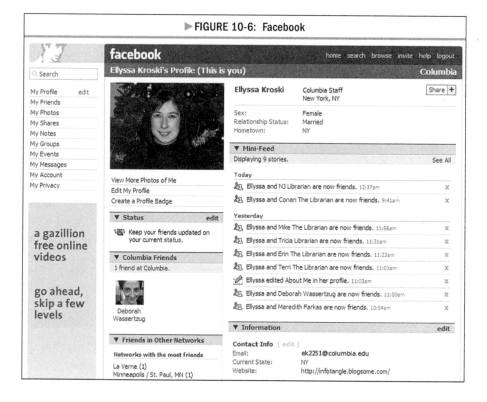

▶FIGURE 10-6: Facebook

SOCIAL NETWORKING WEB SITES

MySpace
www.myspace.com

MySpace is the leading social networking Web site on the Internet today. Owned by News Corp., it boasts over 130 million members. Within this Web community, members can blog, post photos and videos, join groups, and customize their user profiles. Members can discover new filmmakers, musicians, and comedians who have a presence within the community, as well as listen to hundreds of thousands of free songs and watch thousands of video clips.

Facebook
www.facebook.com

Facebook is a social networking community geared toward colleges and universities. Its 19 million members can share photos and videos, customize user profiles, and join over 47,000 different networks or groups. Facebook offers members refined privacy features, which permits them to limit who can find their profiles when conducting searches, and to hide selected information and user-generated content. This social realm enables members to integrate third-party applications, such as Flickr and del.icio.us, into their profiles through their Facebook Applications feature.

Bebo
www.bebo.com

Bebo is the largest social networking Web site in Ireland and New Zealand, and rivals MySpace in the U.K. A similar environment to MySpace, Bebo allows their 31 million members to set up photo albums, upload photos, blog, and create lists of friends. Members can discover any of the 120,000 musical artists who have profiles within the community, as well as connect with college friends.

Orkut
www.orkut.com

Tremendously popular in Brazil, Orkut lays claim to over 37 million registered users, 8 million of whom are Brazilian. This Google social network enables its members to join communities, customize user profiles, and create bookmarks and photo galleries.

Niche Social Networking Web Sites

LinkedIn
www.linkedin.com

Over 10 million professionals are registered members in this networking community for the business world. Members connect to trusted business contacts to create a network. They can then view and be introduced to the people who are in their connections' networks as well.

Maya's Mom
www.mayasmom.com

An online community for parents, Maya's Mom provides a members-only answers service that enables parents to ask and answer each other's questions about children. Members can journal, join groups, upload photos and videos, and create and view activities for children in their area.

Dogster
www.dogster.com

There are over 280,000 registered members within this canine social networking environment. Dog owners can create a page dedicated to their pride and joy, including photo galleries and personal information such as best tricks, favorite toy, and pet-peeves. Members can join groups, leave other dogs a bone, and chat in the doggie forum.

Eons
www.eons.com

A social network for the 50-plus generation, Eons has over 50,000 members who create lists of life dreams, join groups, record their life stories, chat in forums, and read obituaries. Members can create their own blogs and photo albums, and rate media such as television, books, and movies.

Meetup
www.meetup.com

Over 2 million people have become members of this event-driven social networking community. Meetup enables members to find groups of people in their area who share their interests and gives them the tools to organize and meet locally. A means of bringing virtual community into the real world, Meetup groups range from shared hobbies, such as sewing or scrapbooking, to professional and political affiliations.

BEST PRACTICES

▶ **Make Friends**. Social networks are a useful tool for raising consumer aware-ness of your organization and building brand loyalty. However, marketing in these new social networking communities is not about targeting an anony-mous demographic, but rather about forming relationships with people. One way to do that is by making friends in these social networks. For librarians who are social networking, "friend" some people you have something in common with—you never know what other interests you might share. The bottom line is that there is little point in joining a social networking commu-nity if you do not want to be social!

▶ **Spice Up Your Profile**. Your profile gives other people in the community a glimpse into who you are and what you are about. It is your online identity and your virtual image, so make the most out of it. A blank profile is uninter-esting—upload photos of staff members, post library video clips, choose a complementary background, ask friends to come by and leave comments.

▶ **Offer Something Useful**. Online brochures went out of style in the 1990s, and users will not stick around if you do not offer them something of value. Think about what services you could offer to your patrons within these Web sites and try to create something that they might want to tell their friends about. Aim for something viral—something that they can download and put up on their profile, or blog, or Web site that might make other people who see it want to check out your profile. Think about library badges, book widgets, OPAC search tools, etc.

▶ **Engage People**. Capture the attention of social networking users by engaging them in a conversation, or in a creative process. Post polls, ask questions, encourage readers to leave comments on your blog posts, photos, videos, and profile. Tell them about local events or news that they would not find elsewhere.

▶ **Respond to Users**. If you are encouraging your patrons to leave comments and offer feedback, you will want to respond in a timely manner and let them know that someone is listening on your end. It does not need to be a lengthy response, but just enough to let the contributor know that their feed-back is valued.

▶ **Keep Updated**. You do not ever want your profile to look abandoned, so be sure to set realistic goals at the outset. Do not start an events calendar if you do not have the time to update it. Do not start a new blog on MySpace if you already have a library blog and will not have the time to post regularly. In-stead, use the MySpace blog to cross-market your library blog by repurposing

(Cont'd.)

BEST PRACTICES *(Continued)*

---

your material and linking back to the full posts on your original blog. Web site communities such as MySpace offer exposure to millions of readers and can be used as a vehicle to drive traffic not only to your library Web site and online catalog, but to your blog as well!

▶ **Market Your Profile**. Help your library patrons find your profile within the social networking community you have joined. Link to your profile page on your library Web site, add the URL to your next batch of print bookmarks, and print it on your library orientation handouts and workshop materials along with your other contact information.

REFERENCES

Hof, Robert D. "There's Not Enough 'Me' in MySpace." *BusinessWeek* (December 4, 2006). Available: www.businessweek.com/magazine/content/06_49/b4012057.htm?campaign_id=rss_tech (accessed December 4, 2006).

Lenhart, Amanda, and Susannah Fox. "Bloggers: A Portrait of the Internet's New Storytellers." *Pew Internet & American Life Project* (July 19, 2006), p. 14. Available: www.pewinternet.org/pdfs/PIP%20Bloggers%20Report%20July%2019%202006.pdf (accessed December 12, 2006).

Lipsman, Andrew. "More Than Half of MySpace Visitors Are Now Age 35 or Older, as the Site's Demographic Composition Continues to Shift." *ComScore* (October 5, 2006). Available: www.comscore.com/press/release.asp?press=1019 (accessed December 10, 2006).

▶11

VERTICAL SEARCH ENGINES

Thousands of interactive Web 2.0 outlets are enabling businesses, organizations, and individuals to create content on a mammoth scale. In response, a new and focused breed of search engines has appeared to help sift through the wealth of information available on today's Web. Attuned to one niche area, such as blogs, images, electronics, or video, vertical search engines offer their users an in-depth knowledge and a thorough semantic understanding of a particular subject area.

Vertical search engines (VSEs) search the Web for results from a specific market or business sector. By narrowing their search radius and concentrating their subject knowledge, they are able to deliver efficient and highly relevant results sets to their users. In order to achieve this, VSEs utilize a range of proprietary methods. Some of these approaches include developing specialized vocabularies that improve search algorithms, and creating lists of authoritative Web sites that are given added weight during searches. Some media-related search engines implement speech, facial, and pattern recognition technologies to search through photos, videos, and audio files. VSEs attempt to present information to searchers in a robust interface that is well-organized and easy to navigate. Some are offering results in clustered subcategories, and others are presenting previews of linked pages.

Vertical search engines have appeared for major industries and content zones, such as travel, health, and classifieds, and are joined by new tools regularly. Internet searchers are traveling to Farecast to find cheap airfare, to Singingfish and Blinkx seeking videos, Acoona for business queries, Kosmix for health info, and Podzinger to locate podcasts.

Real-time vertical search engine Technorati searches the Web's 75 million blogs to return blog posts created only minutes before. It provides a comprehensive portal to the blogosphere, which receives over 3 million page views per month. Major Web portals such as Google and Yahoo! have identified the value in this class of focused search tool and have joined the market—Google with engines dedicated to blog search and locating multimedia files, and Yahoo! with verticals for jobs, audio, and images. According to a report by Outsell, the vertical search market will top $1 billion in revenue by the year 2009 (Richard, 2006).

VSEs strive to provide comprehensive coverage for their specialized topics and hope to triumph over traditional engines by presenting the user with a complete, portal-like experience.

INSIDE A VERTICAL SEARCH ENGINE

Technorati is a blog search engine that indexes the blogosphere. It updates every few minutes, enabling people to track the conversations happening throughout the Web at any given time. As many of today's vertical search engines do, Technorati attempts to be a one-stop shop for all things related to its topic area. It offers its users various search options, an overview of what is popular, and tools to create customized reports and favorites lists.

Watchlists enable members to save their searches and create customized research pages with RSS feeds. Watchlists created for keyword searches will continually update as new blog posts are made pertaining to that term, while URL-based watchlists will update when new posts are made referencing those blogs. Watchlists update once per hour.

Favorites are lists of bookmarked blogs, which can be organized by members using descriptive tags. Each blog's information page tallies the number of members who have made that blog a favorite.

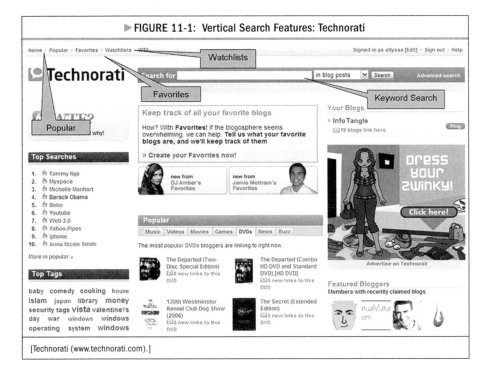

▶FIGURE 11-1: Vertical Search Features: Technorati

[Technorati (www.technorati.com).]

Popular items, such as top tags and popular music, DVDs, and games that bloggers are linking to, are displayed on the front page of Technorati. However, additional lists may be found on the Popular page, which presents the top searches, blogs, videos, movie, and news tracked within the blogosphere, as well as the most favorited blogs.

The **Keyword Search** functionality on Technorati allows users to conduct queries for terms appearing within the full-text of blog posts throughout the Internet. Basic keyword, tag, and directory queries can be performed within the main search box, and limited Boolean queries can be conducted utilizing a search form on the Advanced Search screen.

The **URL Search** option enables visitors to look up the address of any blog to discover what other people are saying about it. This type of search will retrieve blog posts that mention and link to the queried Web address, and acts much like a cited reference search.

Tag Searches on Technorati will seek out blog posts, throughout the Web, which have been assigned that category term. These searches also will retrieve items possessing the tag from other social Web sites, such as Flickr (photos), YouTube (videos), Last.fm (music), and from within its own community (people).

▶ FIGURE 11-2: Vertical Search Features: Technorati Search Page

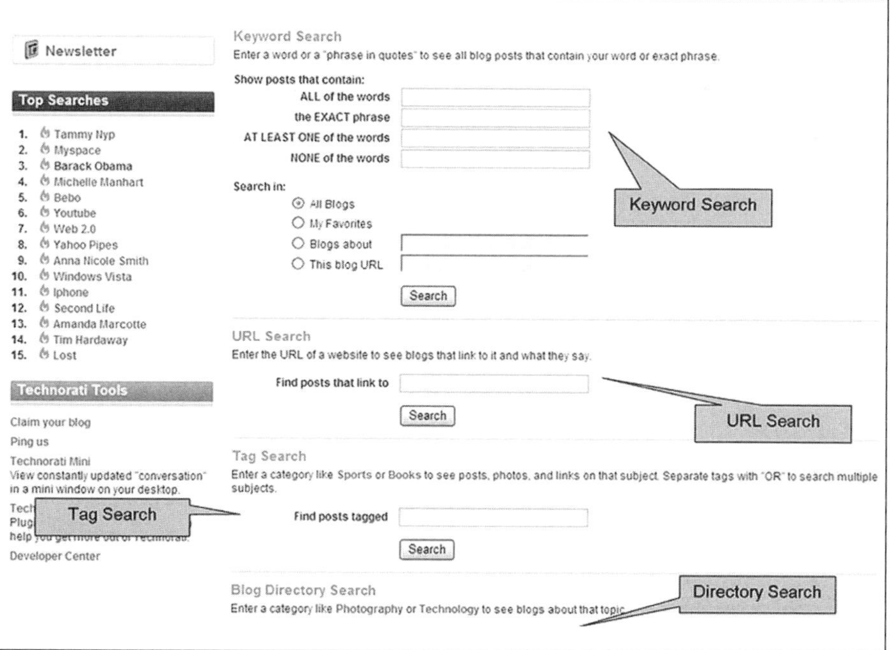

[Technorati (www.technorati.com).]

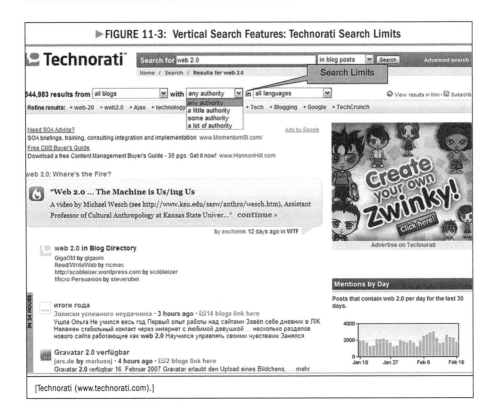

► FIGURE 11-3: Vertical Search Features: Technorati Search Limits

[Technorati (www.technorati.com).]

Directory Searches may be conducted to locate blogs categorized by a particular topic within the Technorati directory. The blog directory also may be browsed to discover new resources within specific subject areas.

Search Limits can be placed on results sets to filter findings by language and by "authority." Authority is a gauge used by Technorati to track the popularity and influence of individual blogs. The search engine measures and assigns authority based on how many blogs link back to a particular Weblog, much like Google's PageRank system.

VERTICAL SEARCH POTENTIAL IN LIBRARIES

Librarians have traditionally provided a portal between people and information. In the age of Web 2.0, they have an opportunity to continue to serve in this capacity by continually seeking out new ways to access information. With the proliferation of content on the World Wide Web, savvy search engines are slicing off subsets of information to focus on. It is through these vertical search engines that libraries and librarians can sort through today's burgeoning online resources and provide a much needed service to their patrons.

▶FIGURE 11-4: Library & Information Science Search Engine (LISZen)

LISZen

www.liszen.com

LISZen is a vertical search engine for the library and information science realm. Created by a library school student, Garrett Hungerford, LISZen is powered by Google Co-op, a tool that enables users to create personalized search engines. This custom VSE keeps tabs on discussions in the biblioblogosphere by searching over 700 library blogs. Blog authors range in specialization from children's librarians at public libraries to corporate librarians in the aerospace industry. While the majority of indexed Weblogs are from English-speakers, over 7 percent are written in other languages such as Turkish, Swedish, Danish, and Japanese. Search results on LISZen can be refined to include only individual blogs or those from special, academic, or school libraries.

Other Ways Libraries Can Use Vertical Search

Subject Search

Librarians can draw on vertical search engines to provide patrons with specialized tools to locate resources within a specific subject area.

Web 2.0 Search

Vertical searches can be employed by librarians to locate blog posts, images, videos, and other rapidly updating Web content that may not be indexed as efficiently through traditional search engines.

Deep Web Search

Librarians can utilize vertical search engines to conduct searches of the Deep or Invisible Web, which includes information and content not usually indexed by traditional search engines. These new search engines may prove more useful when trying to locate such resources, especially content not based on text, such as video files, etc.

Customized Search

Libraries and librarians can utilize vertical search technology to create their own customized finding aids of library-related resources.

Learn from New Technology

Libraries have an opportunity to learn about the advanced search technology employed by some of the latest vertical search engines, such as pattern recognition. They can consider how these may be useful for their own non-text collections.

VERTICAL SEARCH ENGINES

There are hundreds of vertical search engines available on the Web, ranging in scope from Zillow's real estate search, SimplyHired's job seeking tool, and Podzinger's podcast finder to generational searches such as Quintura Kids and Cranky, a search engine aimed at the 50-plus community. Here are just a few others.

Blogs

Technorati

www.technorati.com

Tracking over 75 million blogs, Technorati is the leading search engine for this vertical space. They offer multiple search options as well as the ability to save searches and favorite blogs. They provide top lists, most popular items, and a directory.

Others: Ask Blogs, Google Blog Search, Bloglines

Library

LISZen

www.liszen.com

One of a handful of new search engines designed for the library field, LISZen is the most comprehensive, searching over 700 sources and allowing some filtering options.

Others: LibWorm, Librarian's E-Library

Images

Microsoft Live Image Search

http://search.live.com

Microsoft's Live Image Search offers a gateway to the Web's images through an enhanced, dynamic interface. This slick Web search presents users with image previews, related terms, and a toolbar to zoom and adjust image sizes.

Others: Google Image Search, Yahoo! Image Search, Flickr, Snap, Like, Pixsy

Video

AOL Video

http://video.aol.com

AOL's video search finds videos from all over the Web, including YouTube, MySpace, ESPN, CNN, NBC, and many others. Their search is powered by Truveo, a video search technology that AOL acquired in 2006. Truveo utilizes not only video metadata, but also analyzes text surrounding video files to make retrieval more effective.

Others: Yahoo! Video, YouTube, Google Video, Blinkx, PureVideo, Singingfish

Electronics

Retrevo

www.retrevo.com

Retrevo is a consumer electronics research tool. It indexes reviews and articles about electronic gadgets, including blog posts and photographs, and offers links to shopping sites. Retrevo also searches and provides product manuals and user guides for items.

Others: ViewScore, Wize

Health

Kosmix

www.kosmix.com

Kosmix is a health-related search engine that clusters results into useful subcategories such as causes, symptoms, treatments, and support groups. They also have subdivisions by demographics, including women, men, kids, and a separate subsection geared toward medical professionals, which highlights clinical trials and medical guidelines. Kosmix indexes over 3.2 billion Web pages.

Others: Healia, Healthline

Programming Code

Krugle

www.Krugle.com

A search engine for programmers, Krugle retrieves code snippets from millions of project files for inquiring developers. Searchers can select programming language and project specifications for queries. All code segments that are retrieved include information about the projects they are sourced from and display the document's place within the project directory. Users can browse code documents by project.

Others: AllTheCode, Koders

PERSONALIZED VERTICALS

An emerging type of VSE that is gaining popularity is the personalized search engine. New tools have developed that enable people to create their own search engines quickly and easily without any programming knowledge. Through applications such as Rollyo, Google Co-op, and others, people are creating subject-specific search engines by designating lists of approved Web sites for exploration. These customized searchers also are referred to as social search engines, as they add human filters to the search equation.

A Rollyo Quicktake

www.rollyo.com

Rollyo is a creative abbreviation of "Roll Your Own Search Engine," and it is also a personalized search engine generator. Over 150,000 search engines have been created through this social Web site. Although each interface looks a bit different, most custom search engine tools work the same way.

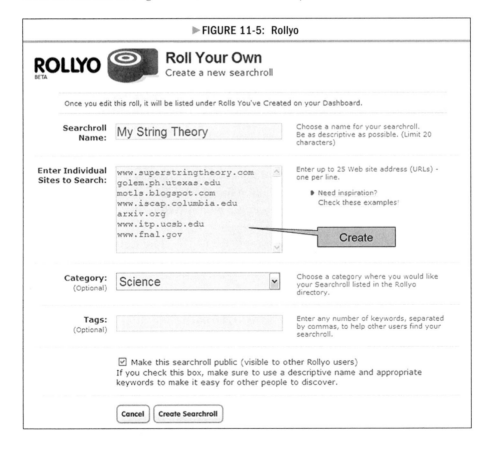

►FIGURE 11-5: Rollyo

To **Create** a new searchroll it is as easy as listing Web site URLs to be searched. Rollyo provides more than 50 starter search engines such as this one (Figure 11-5) on String Theory. Users can customize the search engine by renaming it and adding or subtracting Web sites from the list of sources to search. Since Rollyo is a community Web site as well as a creation tool, members can explore and edit the searchrolls of others. Search rolls may be made public or kept private.

Other Personalized Search Engine Tools

Swicki

http://swicki.eurekster.com

Eurekster's Swicki is a personalized search engine that is trained to perform relevant searches based on types of Web sites specified, as well as on user behavior. These search engines learn and constantly adapt, adding relevant Web sites and weighting search results based on behavior patterns of the community. Nearly 50,000 of these search swickis have been created.

Google Co-op

www.google.com/coop

Google allows users to create their own search engines through the Google Co-op by simply providing a list of Web sites to be searched. Search engine creators can choose to display Google Ad-Sense advertisements on results pages to earn revenue from page views. Within the first six months of releasing the program to the public, over 100,000 custom search engines were created (Enge, 2007).

Yahoo! Search Builder

http://builder.search.yahoo.com

Yahoo!'s custom search builder enables Web site owners to create branded search engines for their sites. Search builders can specify particular Web sites to search, as well as keywords. A tag cloud containing the most popular searches can be included below the search box. Search engines may be tailored to complement an existing Web site theme by customizing font sizes, colors, and types, as well as inserting a logo.

BEST PRACTICES

▶ **Choose the Right Tool for the Job**. There are many different types of search engines available today, and some of them are more effective than others. Spend some time exploring these new applications to determine which provide a more focused search for your most-searched subjects. A good tip is first to locate a search tool that specializes in the format you are looking for, and then use it to search by subject. Many of the larger search engines have verticals that search by format, such as Ask Blog Search, Yahoo! Images, Google Video, etc.

▶ **Create Your Own Search Engine**. As librarians, we are experts at identifying Web sites with authority and solid content, and each of us has a list of trusted sources that we refer to regularly. Instead of visiting each of those Web sites individually and searching for relevant content, why not create a customized search engine that queries all of them?

▶ **Look for New Search Options**. Although some of today's new search engines limit the use of Boolean search operators, or truncation, there are some very useful new search options to be discovered, which can be quite effective. The blog search feature of the Bloglines news reader allows users to limit searches to include only results from the feeds, or blogs to which they are subscribed. This particularly useful feature creates a results list from your handpicked directory of trusted blogs. You also can restrict results to the feeds or news sources subscribed to by another user. Because of the widespread popularity of the Creative Commons license, Google now offers a Usage Rights advanced search feature that enables users to search for images, video clips, movies, books, and educational resources that can be shared and modified. Be on the lookout for these newly available search options.

REFERENCES

Enge, Eric. "Interview of Google's Rajat Mukherjee." *Stone Temple Consulting* (April 16, 2007). Available: www.stonetemple.com/articles/interview-rajat-mukherjee.shtml (accessed April 18, 2007).

Richard, Chuck. "HotTopics: Vertical Search Delivers What Big Search Engines Miss." *Outsell, Inc.* (August 18, 2006). Available: www.outsellinc.com/store/products/289 (accessed January 12, 2007).

▶12

SOCIAL NEWS

There is a monumental shift taking place in the world of news today: a grass-roots revolution that is rapidly changing the way that news is distributed and consumed on the Web. Traditionally, the news has been chosen for the reader by a small group of editors, but new social news aggregators are transforming conventional notions about content delivery by shifting the selection of newsworthy stories from the few to the many. Social news Web sites enable the community to become the editor, leaving the crucial decisions about what appears on the "front page" up to the readers. They are an evolution of Web sites, such as Slashdot, which has allowed readers to submit stories and comment on them since the late 1990s. Today's social news applications are seeing readers creating, ranking, and discovering top news stories and sharing them with others. Akin to other Web 2.0 technologies, community-driven news Web sites uproot established paradigms in favor of a bottom-up approach that offers the masses the opportunity to decide what is important.

Social news aggregation Web sites empower their members to submit, vote for, and comment on news stories from anywhere on the Web in a centralized forum. Individual news items are voted on and ranked according to popularity on Web sites such as Digg, reddit, and Netscape. The stories that the community deems the most noteworthy, as reflected by the number of positive endorsements, are displayed on the front page. Readers are able to track stories, topics, and other members via RSS and other tools.

This DIY model of news readership has had such an astounding appeal to Internet users that traffic on these social news Web sites has begun to rival that of old media stalwarts. With more traffic than the *Washington Post* and *USA Today*, the popularity of the social news Web site Digg approaches and at times surpasses that of *The New York Times*. Over 1 million people visit this peer-filtered news site daily to "digg" for stories, rendering it the twenty-first most popular Web site amongst U.S. users.

Web 2.0 users need not wait to be told what news is important to them; they can determine that for themselves. Readers can now interact directly with their news, providing instant feedback in the form of user comments and voting. This democ-ratization of news delivery embraces the power of the many and unseats the media elite, placing the reins of control firmly into the hands of the reader.

ANATOMY OF A SOCIAL NEWS AGGREGATOR

There is a multitude of social news Web sites available online today, each with a customized interface and design, but there are several features that are commonly found in most of them.

News Stories are the main elements on social news sites. They are displayed in order of popularity down the center of the Web site. Each story includes informa-tion about the number of votes, or **diggs**, it has received from the community, the news source from which the story is linked, the member who submitted it, and how long ago it was posted to the site.

The **diggs** tally includes the total number of positive votes a news story has earned; diggs may also be referred to as votes, points, and/or shouts in other community news environments.

The **digg it** function allows members to vote for or endorse a news story. By clicking the "digg it" or vote button, readers are actively contributing to the content that will appear on the Web site. Stories that do not receive a high number

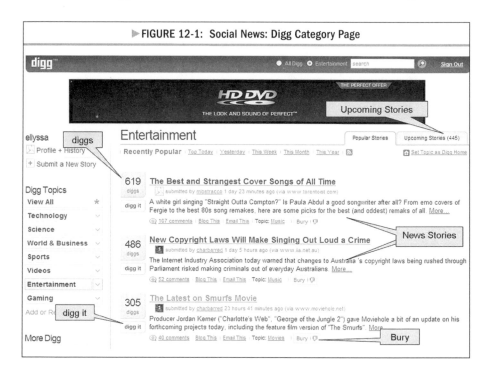

▶FIGURE 12-1: Social News: Digg Category Page

of diggs, or are ignored ("buried") by users, do not appear on the main "popular" pages of the Web site. Although they are archived and remain searchable, they remain obscure and undiscovered by the greater part of the community.

Bury is an option that enables members to demote news stories and/or report problems such as spam, duplicate news items, or broken links.

Upcoming Stories is the temporary holding area for newly submitted stories. Many of these social news Web sites employ such a queue where new postings reside for up to 24 hours, awaiting votes. Such systems leverage the wisdom of crowds to decide what is displayed on the main page. News stories that receive a comparably high number of votes are promoted to the front page.

The **Submit** a New Story function allows members of the community to post a news item to the Web site for others to vote on. This is a simple process on these Web sites, which involves little more than linking to the story and providing a title. This low barrier to entry makes participation possible even for a tech novice. News fans will find "digg this story" and "add to reddit" options spreading across an increasing number of major media sites such as the *Washington Post* and *The New York Observer.*

Comments are an integral component of social news applications. They empower users to provide immediate reactions to and opinions about news stories.

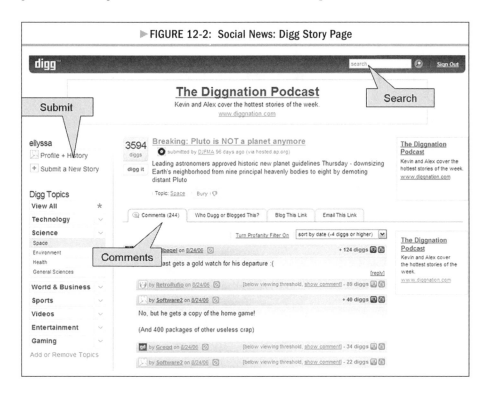

▶ FIGURE 12-2: Social News: Digg Story Page

Many major media Web sites still do not allow their readers to comment on stories. Community-driven news Web sites offer their members the opportunity to discuss what they are reading in a centralized space.

Search enables users to access archived news stories. Some of these sites offer advanced search functionality that permits searching by tags, users, or front-page stories.

SOCIAL NEWS POTENTIAL IN LIBRARIES

Social news aggregation Web sites represent a pioneering new trend in the distribution of news online. These Web 2.0 applications give readers a voice and empower them to contribute to the process of disseminating the news. Libraries and librarians, who are in the business of disseminating news and information to their patrons, may find it beneficial to take note of this increasingly popular development.

Librarians who wish to find patrons where they "live" will be most interested in becoming members of these communities. Not only will joining these Web sites present an opportunity to learn about how users prefer to receive news and information, but will provide insight into what makes communities like these so popular.

Lipstick.com Implementation
http://lipstick.com

Media giant Condé Nast has implemented the social news aggregation model on its celebrity gossip Web site, Lipstick.com. Within this beta site, Condé Nast has

▶ FIGURE 12-3: Lipstick.com

customized the appearance of the reddit technology to integrate within their brand. They have left the task of gathering and organizing news content to their readers who are encouraged to post celebrity-related news items found throughout the Internet. Just as on the original reddit.com Web site, members vote for and against stories that shuffle up and down the ranks accordingly. By doing this, Condé Nast is able to offer their readers a fully interactive and dynamic news experience while maintaining the feeling of their brand.

Other Ways Libraries Can Use Social News Technology

Keep Current

Librarians can use these Web sites to keep up to date about breaking news in a variety of fields. Since these sites harness the collective intelligence, librarians can view at a glance what the most popular or important stories are at any given time.

Outreach

Libraries that provide news for their patrons could create library user profiles offering links to current global news stories that librarians have endorsed.

Library Communities

Libraries and librarians in similar fields could collaborate to create communities within these Web sites by linking user profiles via the "friends" feature.

Gain Insight into User Behavior

Social news Web sites are news aggregation sources; they are new resources that users are tapping to find information about current events. Libraries and librarians will want to be aware of these. Through them, libraries can gain insight into the elements that make these rapidly growing social news communities so successful, such as: the self-service model, low learning curve, simplicity of design and function, trust, democratic character, social nature, and participatory features.

Learn from New Technology

Libraries can utilize these Web sites as an opportunity to learn about the methods by which users prefer to consume and disseminate news online. This new method includes user participation and mixes media types and formats to present the user with news stories from blogs, newspapers, magazines, podcasts, photos, and videos.

Create Similar Tools

Technologically gifted libraries could create similar tools, or partner with software companies, to offer comparable functionality on their own Web sites.

SOCIAL NEWS AGGREGATION TECHNOLOGY

Digg

http://digg.com

A Silicon Valley venture, Digg was the first major application to offer social news aggregation of this kind and is generally considered a leader in this space. The majority of its one million registered users tend toward the technology-inclined, even though Digg expanded to non-tech subject areas in June 2006. Digg offers users several views of its content, including popular and upcoming stories, a browsable monthly archive, and the Digg Spy tool—a real-time display of the activity on the Web site. Digg has issued a free public API available for users and partners to access its data dating back to 2004.

reddit

http://reddit.com

Boston-based startup reddit was purchased by mainstream media company Condé Nast, which utilizes this community-moderated news technology on its lipstick.com property. reddit received over one million unique visitors per month prior to the acquisition and continues to license its software to media companies such as Gawker Media and the *Washington Post*–owned *Slate Magazine*. Reddit allows users to both promote and demote stories, save stories, and sort news items by controversy.

Netscape

www.netscape.com

With topic channels ranging from autos to religion, Netscape.com is a social news aggregation Web site targeted at the mainstream user. The AOL-owned portal utilizes editors, called anchors, who moderate its social news community. Readers retain the ability to submit, comment, and vote on stories as on other social news Web sites, but the activity within is monitored. Netscape provides a leader board— a listing of top contributors—a live site activity tracker, and related stories.

Topix

www.topix.net

A leading news gathering Web site that enables its community to contribute as local editors, Topix.net is a hybrid social news aggregator. It combines the traditional news delivery model with a sprinkling of new social and citizen journalism features. Topix is funded by the Tribune, Gannett, and McClatchy media companies and provides news to such online publications as the *LA Times* and the *Chicago Tribune*. Founded by the creators of the DMOZ, a human-powered Web directory also known as the Open Directory Project, Topix aggregates news from over 50,000 sources, a number which is seven times that of Yahoo! News. Members can create, submit, and comment on news stories, as well as discuss them at length in the community forums.

Newsvine

www.newsvine.com

Founded by professionals from ESPN, Disney, and other mainstream media companies, the Seattle-based Newsvine is a major competitor in the realm of social news. Newsvine's offerings are a unique amalgamation of social news aggregation features and citizen journalism. The site syndicates news items from the Associated Press (AP) to members who vote on them, along with stories that they submit, or "seed," themselves. Readers also are encouraged to create their own news items by starting a news column. Ad revenue is earned by traffic to members' original and seeded stories. Newsvine offers watchlists, local and regionalized news, live chat, and a conversation tracker.

CITIZEN JOURNALISM

In addition to developments in news delivery and consumption, Web 2.0 facilitates changes in the way news is created. The previously well-marked lines between reader and author have become increasingly blurred with the advent of the participatory Web. New citizen journalism Web sites have begun to gain traction as an alternative, "power to the people" approach to news. Eyewitness contributors have been acknowledged for their coverage of major news events from hurricane Katrina, to the 2004 Indonesian tsunami, to the London terrorist bombings of 2005. Ordinary people have joined to become an army of amateur reporters, which rivals that of traditional media with regard to speed, breadth of coverage, and sheer numbers. The Associated Press, the backbone of the world's news system, employs 3,700 staff members worldwide, while the Seoul-based grassroots newsforce at OhmyNews boasts over 43,000 global citizen reporters at their disposal posting 200 articles per day.

The popularity of user-contributed content has not been lost on major media companies. Gannett Co., owner of 90 American newspapers including *USA Today*, will begin incorporating citizen journalism efforts into its publications. CNN has created its own citizen-contributor Web site at CNN Exchange, which features user-generated articles, photos, videos, and audio files. The *International Herald Tribune* has provided financial backing for OhMyNews, and Reuters news agency has partially funded the citizen journalism effort New Assignment.net.

The best-known citizen journalism sites are:

OhmyNews: http://english.ohmynews.com
NowPublic: www.nowpublic.com
Citizenbay: www.citizenbay.com
NewAssignment.net: http://newassignment.wordpress.com

MEMETRACKERS

Memetrackers track what the blogosphere is saying about major news stories. A meme is a contagious idea, concept, or line of thought that is passed from person to person, evolving as it persists. These Web sites display the hottest news items being discussed by bloggers within minutes of their posts. The first and leading tracker of Weblog conversations, Techmeme, scans thousands of blogs and major news Web sites and automatically updates every five minutes. Users can view snapshots of what was hot at any point in time by accessing its archives.

The best-known memetracker sites are:

Techmeme: www.techmeme.com
Tailrank: http://tailrank.com
Megite: www.megite.com

BEST PRACTICES

▶ **Offer Links**. Outfit your blog with links to social news Web sites, such as Digg and reddit, to make it easy for your readers to submit your news items. These links should appear below or beside your blog posts, along with other links to major bookmarking tools such as del.icio.us, etc.

▶ **Become a User**. Use these new technologies to stay current but also to learn what makes them work for millions of users. Discover why this is the preferred method of news consumption for so many people and whether this is the type of news delivery service you would like to incorporate into your own Web site community.

►13

ANSWERS TECHNOLOGY

This next phase of Web development is an era of information democracy—a time when everyone has the ability to create and share information and experience with their peers. New Questions & Answers services seek to bring out the expert in all of us while creating a global database of the world's knowledge. Tapping the power of the collective intelligence, these Q&A sites embrace the philosophy that the many are more knowledgeable than the one. Leveraging the efforts of the community, they provide users with a wealth of peer-generated content and a social experience.

This new technology trend allows people to pose questions to the community, answer others' queries, and browse resolved inquiries. These systems rely on people's increasing trust in their peers, as well as their inclination to access information freely and according to their schedules. This self-service model is bolstered by the users' ability to not only contribute to and expand their community, but to influence its integrity. A keen system of checks and balances exists on these Web sites in the form of ratings and reputation systems. Users rate questions, answers, and other users according to their quality and have the ability to report inappropriate behavior. They are also able to track activity and people in the community through RSS feeds and other tools.

Yahoo!, Microsoft, and Amazon have all joined the fray, along with a number of other independent competitors. Yahoo! Answers garnered over 160 million answers within the first year of its inception in December 2005 and has become the second most popular online reference site behind Wikipedia. The popular social Q&A Web site is host to over 60 million monthly visitors—not a small number compared to the 72 million who frequent the mega video-sharing enterprise YouTube each month.

Users are posting questions ranging from "Which herbs grow best indoors?" to "Where can I get good Mac & Cheese in NYC?" and some dedicated answerers have posted over 5,000 responses to queries. While an average question receives approximately eight answers, a posting by renowned physicist Stephen Hawking has reaped over 25,000 responses.

The Web now follows television and newspapers as the third most visited source that people turn to for information. Today's information seekers are turning to social networks to act as filters for information quality. It is not the "experts" who hold sway with today's Web user, when it comes to company information, but rather a "person like me" who has been found to be the most credible source, according to Edelman trust surveys (Edelman, 2006). As trust in traditional authorities wanes, so increases peer reliance.

INSIDE ANSWERS SERVICES

Although there are various answers services available today, they share many of the same features and interface elements.

Questions are one-half of the attraction on these Q&A Web sites. They can be posted by any registered member and likewise be answered by any. Members can browse open or resolved questions, answer open questions, or vote for the best answer to a specific query, most often within the main portion of the site.

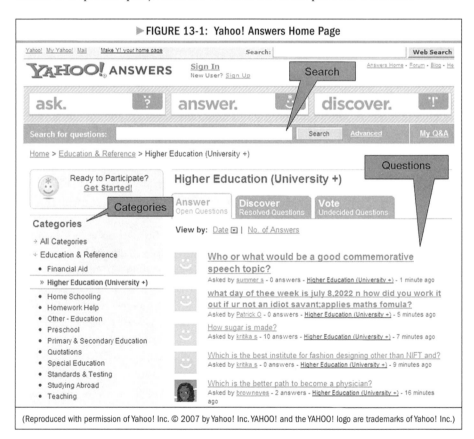

▶FIGURE 13-1: Yahoo! Answers Home Page

(Reproduced with permission of Yahoo! Inc. © 2007 by Yahoo! Inc. YAHOO! and the YAHOO! logo are trademarks of Yahoo! Inc.)

Categories, subcategories, or tags are a basic form of navigation on these sites. Some answers sites have a predetermined set of categories for classification of answers, while others rely on user tagging to develop this system. As people pose new questions, they assign them to a relevant category, or tag them with descriptive keywords.

Search allows members to query for an exact topic of interest. Some of these sites have employed search functionality that permits limiting the results by question status: open questions, resolved questions, most answered questions, etc.

Voting Options are available to users in order to rate the quality of individual answers. The theory with these sites, as with others that tap into the collective intelligence, is that the incorrect and irrelevant will be weeded out by the masses. Options range from selecting one choice for best answer to rating degrees of utility.

Best Answers are the responses that have been voted by the community of users to have addressed most satisfactorily a specific query. They are listed first, directly following their question.

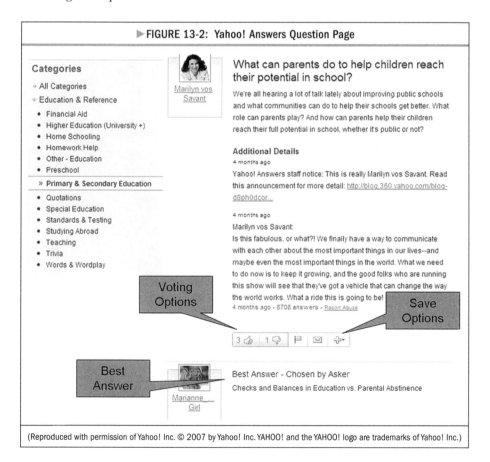

▶ FIGURE 13-2: Yahoo! Answers Question Page

Categories

→ All Categories
↓ Education & Reference
- Financial Aid
- Higher Education (University +)
- Home Schooling
- Homework Help
- Other - Education
- Preschool
» **Primary & Secondary Education**
- Quotations
- Special Education
- Standards & Testing
- Studying Abroad
- Teaching
- Trivia
- Words & Wordplay

Marilyn vos Savant

What can parents do to help children reach their potential in school?

We're all hearing a lot of talk lately about improving public schools and what communities can do to help their schools get better. What role can parents play? And how can parents help their children reach their full potential in school, whether it's public or not?

Additional Details
4 months ago

Yahoo! Answers staff notice: This is really Marilyn vos Savant. Read this announcement for more detail: http://blog.360.yahoo.com/blog-d8ph0dcor...

4 months ago

Marilyn vos Savant:

Is this fabulous, or what?! We finally have a way to communicate with each other about the most important things in our lives--and maybe even the most important things in the world. What we need to do now is to keep it growing, and the good folks who are running this show will see that they've got a vehicle that can change the way the world works. What a ride this is going to be!

4 months ago - 8708 answers - Report Abuse

Voting Options

Save Options

3 👍 1 👎 🏳 ✉ ➕▾

Best Answer

Marianne Girl

Best Answer - Chosen by Asker

Checks and Balances in Education vs. Parental Abstinence

(Reproduced with permission of Yahoo! Inc. © 2007 by Yahoo! Inc. YAHOO! and the YAHOO! logo are trademarks of Yahoo! Inc.)

Save Options available for users vary among different applications; however, most offer RSS feeds to keep users updated about both questions and other members. Other save options may include saving to del.icio.us, Furl, Blinklist, and other social bookmarking Web sites, adding to watchlists, saving to a blog post, or submitting to a news site such as Digg. Some systems offer members RSS feeds for all questions, as well as by category.

Answerer Profiles exist in all answers services and are a means by which other users gauge the authority of the responses that they post. Each user's profile contains statistics demonstrating their performance in answering and in some cases posing queries. By answering questions well, users gain a trustworthy reputation. Alternatively, by answering them poorly, they become known as unreliable. Beside each question and answer is an icon representing the author of that particular content, which leads to that person's profile. This enables members to navigate these systems by users.

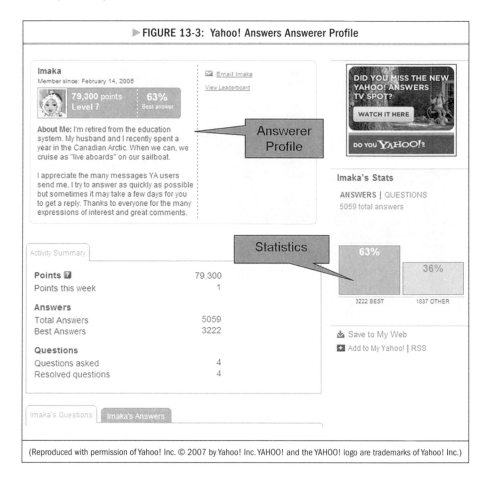

▶ FIGURE 13-3: Yahoo! Answers Answerer Profile

(Reproduced with permission of Yahoo! Inc. © 2007 by Yahoo! Inc. YAHOO! and the YAHOO! logo are trademarks of Yahoo! Inc.)

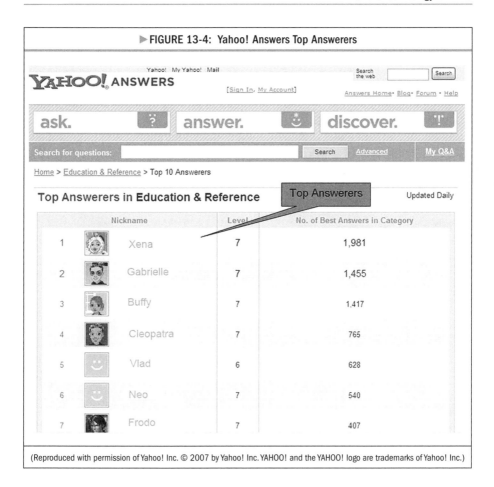

▶FIGURE 13-4: Yahoo! Answers Top Answerers

(Reproduced with permission of Yahoo! Inc. © 2007 by Yahoo! Inc. YAHOO! and the YAHOO! logo are trademarks of Yahoo! Inc.)

Statistics indicate the positive or negative performance of each user. They often will detail how many times they have contributed a "best answer," as well as how many total questions they have asked and/or answered.

Top Answerers often are listed as the top ranked and/or most active participants within these answers sites. These "top" member lists are sometimes referred to as leader boards.

ANSWERS SERVICES POTENTIAL IN LIBRARIES

A great part of the attraction and success of these Q&A services is that they provide information seekers with tacit knowledge that is often difficult to find through traditional search engines. Coincidentally, this also happens to be a major strength of librarians. In addition to many ready-reference questions, users on answers Web sites are asking for assistance with "how-to-find" and "how-to-approach" research queries.

Wherever intellectuals exchange information, it is useful to have guides present, not to intrude but to offer themselves as a resource. This is an opportunity for libraries to go where their patrons are, to learn about their use culture and their information needs firsthand. Not only would a librarian presence in such a community be welcome, it would also present an opportunity for them to learn about user interaction within these communities.

iYogaLife Answerbag Implementation

http://iyogalife.answerbag.com

iYogaLife magazine has integrated Answerbag's technology within their Web site. Using a widget that is freely available to Web site developers, they gained the ability to syndicate Answerbag's questions and answers within their own customized templates. By implementing the Answerbag functionality within their Web site, *iYogaLife* is able to offer their readers a self-service reference tool without creating any content themselves and still maintaining the look and feel of their brand. They can direct their readers to focused Q&A categories that complement their site content, such as yoga, Pilates, dieting and nutrition, etc. Their readers are

▶ FIGURE 13-5: iYogaLife Answerbag

able to access and participate in a questions-and-answers service from within *iYogaLife*'s site, providing them with a seamless experience.

Professor X—Stellar Answerer

http://tinyurl.com/3e37tk

Professor X is a Director of Graduate Studies at a prominent university. She is also a valued answerer within the Yahoo! Answers community. She has provided over 1,800 information seekers with answers pertaining to undergraduate and graduate programs within the United States. Through the Yahoo! Answers site, she provides potential graduate students with advice about admissions essays, faculty recommendations, and choosing the right program. She offers insight into university housing and tips on doctoral dissertations, provides answers to many ready-reference questions, and assists users who are searching for journal articles. Over 1,550 of her answers have been selected by members as the "Best Answer."

Other Ways Libraries Can Use Answers Technology

Create Similar Tools

Libraries can utilize the Answerbag widget or Yahoo! Answers API functionality to create an answers community within their own library's Web site. They can target specific subject areas to support more traditional subject guides or FAQs.

Virtual Reference

Libraries can utilize answers tools within their own library communities and restrict them to controlled user groups, such as student questioners and librarian answerers, in order to offer such a service as an extension of IM and e-mail reference.

Learn from New Technology

Libraries and librarians can make use of these services as an opportunity to learn about patron interests and how they prefer to receive information online. They can use this knowledge to create other "self-service" offerings for their patrons.

Gain Insight into User Behavior

Libraries can utilize these services to gain insight into the types of questions members ask that they may not be answering for their own patrons within a given subject area. Question types may include tacit knowledge queries, such as "What is the best way to go about studying for the GRE," etc.

Outreach

Libraries can take part in these Q&A Web sites in a community outreach effort to not only create a library presence within these social networks, but to provide answers to subject-specific questions.

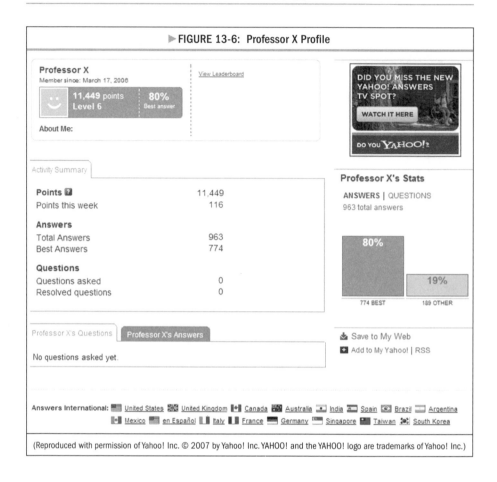

▶FIGURE 13-6: Professor X Profile

(Reproduced with permission of Yahoo! Inc. © 2007 by Yahoo! Inc. YAHOO! and the YAHOO! logo are trademarks of Yahoo! Inc.)

ANSWERS TECHNOLOGY

Yahoo! Answers

http://answers.yahoo.com

This is the leading answers service on the Web today at over 160 million answers and a growth rate of 35 percent per month as of its first year. They offer a wealth of RSS feeds and advance search options, as well as many save and bookmarking choices.

Answerbag

www.answerbag.com

Answerbag was acquired by Demand Media in the fall of 2006. This Q&A service is loaded with features, including the ability to add video clips and photos to answers. They also have more bookmarking and save options than any other service.

Windows QnA Live

http://qna.live.com

Microsoft has joined the fray with this offering. Instead of preset categories, they are letting their users determine the structure of their taxonomy by enabling tagging throughout the site. They offer loads of RSS feeds, as well as IM alerts, to their users.

Yedda

http://yedda.com

Yedda is Hebrew for "knowledge," and it is also an Israeli startup that has developed a powerful answers service. Users interested in answering questions can register for topics within an area of their own expertise for which they can receive notification via e-mail when relevant questions are posted. Yedda offers competitive features and also extends the social aspects of such an environment by allowing users to create friends lists.

Askville

http://askville.amazon.com

Askville is Amazon.com's Q&A property that has a rewards system reminiscent of a role-playing game. Its unique reputation system involves gaining experience points and Quest Coins. Experience points are earned and lost based on the quality of the answers given, and members reach levels of experience reflective of their expertise in an area. Based on their performance on the Web site, with actions such as asking and answering relevant questions, members can earn Quest Coins that can be spent within the Questville.com community.

▶TABLE 13-1: Answers Features Comparison					
Overall	Yahoo! Answers	Answerbag	QnA Live	Yedda	Askville
Categories	■	■			
Tags			■	■	■
Videos		■			■
Photos		■		■	■
Comments	■	■	■	■	■
Advanced Search	■				
Leader Board	■	■	■	■	■
Watch Lists	■	■			■
Bookmarking	■	■		■	
RSS	■	■	■		
IM Alerts			■		
Contacts				■	■
Widget/API	■	■		■	

BEST PRACTICES

▶ **Join the Community**. Immerse yourself in an answers community and contribute responses; tell your patrons that you will be there offering virtual reference help. Discover whether this is a service that both you and your patrons find useful.

REFERENCE

Annual Edelman Trust Barometer 2006. http://www.edelman.com/image/insights/content/ FullSupplement_final.pdf. Viewed 6/5/07

►14

VIRTUAL WORLDS

Virtual worlds are projected to be the wave of the future, and librarians are riding the swell by establishing information outposts within these online environments. One such realm in particular, known as "Second Life," has attracted the energies of hundreds of tech-savvy librarians eager to participate in its strategic life-simulating atmosphere and non-gamelike structure. Although there are many other virtual ecospheres available online, the vast majority of library activity has centered on Second Life, so the discussions in this chapter will focus on that world specifically.

Anything goes in the game of Second Life, where social networking goes 3-D within a massively multiplayer online game (MMOG). Unlike other online games such as "World of Warcraft," Second Life is an immense social community that presents players with none of the familiar ingredients regularly found in these environments, such as treasure chests, epic battles, and goal-oriented quests. Instead, "residents" can read books, meditate, gamble, fly, sell real estate, play musical instruments, or run a business. In this game that is not a game, players take on the personas of their avatars and lead second lives where they can hold jobs, travel the world, make friends, and get an education. Within the Second Life realm, the user experience is limited only by the imagination of the players, who can create not only their own existences, but that of the world around them.

Second Life is a rich and interactive virtual world that has intrigued millions with its open-handed nature and sense of self-determination. Members of Second Life can create and develop the appearance of their own animated avatar that represents them within the community. Through this avatar, players are able to interact with the world around them in many ways, including chatting, talking, flying, teleporting, and exploring. Instead of quests, Second Life offers a free-market economy built on the Linden Dollar, as well as an exchange rate with real-world currency. Players can buy and sell goods and services to make a living both in-world and in RL (real life). Everything within this virtual domain has been created by its inhabitants who retain control over the intellectual property rights of their inventions.

Colleges and universities, including Harvard Law School, are using the virtual realm as an educational platform for remote learning, offering courses ranging from architecture to cyber law. Politicians such as California's George Miller and Mark Warner of Virginia are holding press conferences and giving in-world interviews in Second Life. This rapidly growing gaming phenomenon has drawn over 8 million individuals from all backgrounds, who are screening films, running corporate training sessions, getting married, playing games, exploring foreign lands, and recruiting new employees. Residents of Second Life have gathered together to participate in events as varied as a Darfur rally, a Jay-Z concert, and an MTV fashion show.

Major corporations such as IBM, Sony, Nike, and Warner Brothers have discovered that Second Life offers new opportunities in marketing, branding, training, and conferencing. Government organizations such as the Centers for Disease Control are using it for promotion, while the Department of Homeland Security has practiced emergency response preparedness. Auto moguls Toyota, Nissan, and General Motors are all offering Second Life residents virtual transportation, and media companies such as Reuters, CNet, and *Wired* magazine have set up news bureaus.

Second Life presents limitless business opportunities for both corporations and individuals, as members spend over $1.5 million per day on land and services purchases. Annual audience figures for MMOGs in general are predicted to nearly triple, from the 3.7 million users in 2006 to 9 million in 2011, and annual revenues are forecast to increase from $348 million to $842 million during that same period, according to analysts at Jupiter Research (Gartenberg and Horwitz, 2006).

Straight from the pages of Neal Stephenson's *Snow Crash*, Second Life presents a metaverse, or cyberspace realm in which people connect and socialize through the use of avatars in a virtual reality created by its residents. In this online realm, members are able to interact in new ways, sharing synchronous experiences and information exchanges within a 3-D community space.

FEATURES OF A VIRTUAL WORLD

Second Life is a sophisticated gaming system with many tools and features available to players. While some players will want to master the advanced building tools, learn scripting, or design their own templates, many players are content to learn the basic skills necessary to interact with the world. In Second Life, the experience is up to the individual, and all levels of expertise are embraced. Here is a look at some of the basic features found in the world of Second Life.

The **Build** feature enables players to create and edit the land and objects that appear in-world. Second Life objects are created using geometric primitives, also known as prims, which are shaped, sized, and formatted with the provided 3-D modeling tools. Once objects have been built, animations can be added to them through scripts. Creations can be copied and sold to other residents.

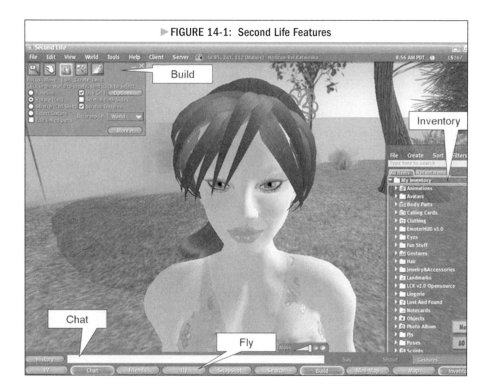

▶FIGURE 14-1: Second Life Features

Inventory items are stored in a folder directory and can be searched, sorted, copied, and deleted. Inventory can be organized by adding new folders or dragging folders into one another. All clothing outfits, hair, skin, body shapes, landmarks, gestures, poses, scripts, notecards, objects, and animations are stored in the inventory.

Flying is one of the major forms of transportation within Second Life. After clicking this command, players can toggle between page-up and page-down buttons to soar through the skies. Members can take in an aerial view throughout the Second Life world, except in specified no-fly zones.

The **Chat** bar enables residents to participate in real-time chat with others who are nearby. Typing a message into this box sends it to all other residents within the immediate vicinity of the sender. A chat history box can be clicked on to keep up with previous and multiple conversations. For private chatter, members can IM individual players who are located throughout the world.

A **Map** of each region or parcel of land within Second Life is provided, which displays events, main information areas, popular places, and the player's location. Green dots on the map indicate other Second Life residents who are currently in that area. Through the map, players can access and view their landmarks and can teleport to any place in the world.

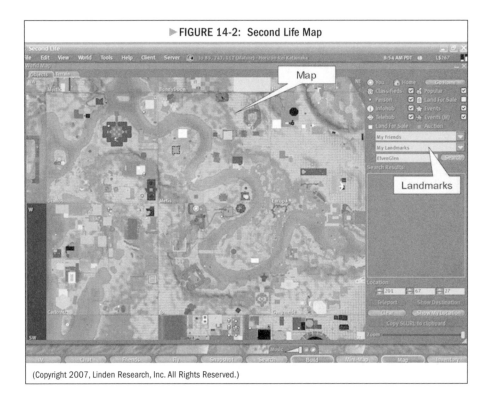

►FIGURE 14-2: Second Life Map

(Copyright 2007, Linden Research, Inc. All Rights Reserved.)

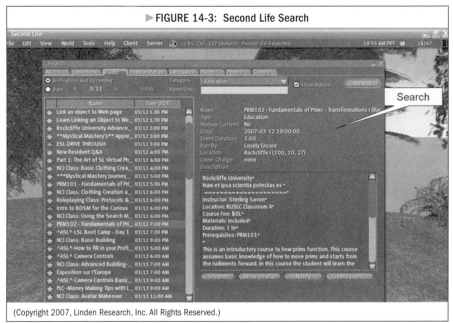

►FIGURE 14-3: Second Life Search

(Copyright 2007, Linden Research, Inc. All Rights Reserved.)

Landmarks are references, or bookmarks, to a particular place. They store the geographic information necessary to locate that area again, including the region and the x, y, and z coordinates on the map. Landmarks can be accessed through the map where members can teleport to these saved places. They also can be retrieved and organized through the inventory folders.

Search allows residents to search for places, people, groups, classifieds, land sales, and events. This is a great starting point for discovering what is happening in-world at any given time. A search of the events tab in the category Education will return pages of class listings for upcoming workshops, along with their time and date, and the option to teleport to the location (see Figure 14-3). Many of these classes are on topics of interest to newcomers, such as introduction to building, working with prims, and designing clothing.

HOW ARE LIBRARIES USING VIRTUAL WORLDS?

Libraries are using Second Life as the new location for the branch library. They are establishing virtual satellite branches in-world to offer online patrons another way to interact with the library. Setting up virtual portals to the real-world library, these outposts provide Second Lifers the opportunity to access library databases, catalogs, and live help from librarians. Libraries are offering in-world tours, classes to learn game skills, bibliographic instruction, and genealogy workshops, as well as creating special exhibits.

Alliance Second Life Library
http://slurl.com/secondlife/Info%20Island/128/128/0

The Alliance Second Life Library hosts nine Information Islands within the virtual world, where they offer library programming, provide tours, present shows, exhibits, and author signings, as well as hold Online Programming for All Libraries (OPAL) training sessions. Their libraries' shelves hold items as diverse as the *2006 Statistical Abstracts*, H.G. Wells' *The Time Machine*, and medical reference sources such as the *Merck Manual*. Avatars visiting the SL library can access research databases and online resources such WorldCat, The Complete Works of Shakespeare, Medline, and dictionaries and encyclopedias such as MSN Encarta. Second Life residents can attend storytelling sessions, book and film discussions, or classes in genealogy, health awareness, and building in Second Life through the Library.

A joint effort between the Alliance Library System, the Charlotte-Mecklenburg County (NC) Library and OPAL, the Second Life Library hopes to fulfill a need for library services in a virtual realm. "We could see that virtual worlds and gaming were growing in popularity and that libraries needed to be there in the beginning to see what services were needed, what could be offered and

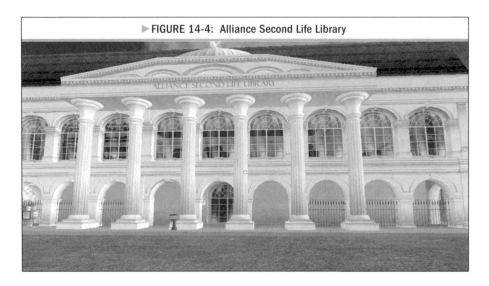

▶FIGURE 14-4: Alliance Second Life Library

in what formats," said Lori Bell, Director of Innovation at the Alliance Library System.

After considering other virtual environments, such as Active Worlds, the team chose to establish a presence in Second Life due to the unlimited opportunities for growth offered by the program and the number of participating educators already in-world. They decided to jump in and start small, announcing their grand opening in October 2006. Many libraries and organizations have since joined them to establish their own in-world presence, such as UCLA and the ALA, and SirsiDynix and Talis have partnered with them as sponsors. The new virtual library organization publicized their progress within a project blog, letting the community know about their efforts and accomplishments.

The Second Life Library has grown from a single island to nine thriving island communities, including a Health Info island with two medical libraries and Edu-Island designed specifically for in-world educators. They have over 75 active librarian volunteers offering reference services, conducting archival work, building collections, and constructing exhibits. They have a greeter present in their welcome area for 40 hours per week. At present, the main Info Island draws over 4,000 visitors daily.

Bell recommends collaborating with other libraries and organizations when planning projects of this scale. "No one person or library could offer the scope of exhibits, programs, etc., that a group of libraries can offer," she commented. The Alliance Second Life Library won second prize in the August 2006 Talis Mashup Competition, and was awarded the ALA/Information Today Library of the Future Award in 2007. (Lori Bell, e-mail correspondence with author, March 2007)

Other Ways Libraries Are Using Virtual Worlds

Library Workshops

The Geneology Center on Info Island provides genealogy research resources for Second Life residents, as well as classes on searching vital records.

In-World Tours

The ICT (Information and Communication Technology) Library on Info Island offers wearable tours of educational sites in Second Life, as well as free scripts and game-related guides.

Special Exhibits

The State Library of Kansas has established a virtual branch within Cybrary City II. They have created an interactive tornado awareness month exhibit with live tornado animations, statistics, Web resources, and images. The Kansas branch also offers state statistical information, access to the statewide catalog, and local history and genealogy resources.

Database and Catalog Access

The Society Hill Branch of the Darlington County Library system in South Carolina maintains a book display in their SL library located in Cybrary City. The display contains book information and links to the titles on Amazon. They also provide access to literary indexes, religious resources, and their library catalog. Also in Cybrary City, the Georgia Institute of Technology Second Life Library provides patrons with access to Georgia Tech dissertations, resource guides, library databases, and the library catalog.

Virtual Reference

McMaster University (ON, Canada) Libraries has a library office in Cybrary City, offering database searching and access to the library catalog, as well as live librarian support.

Library Resources

The Topeka and Shawnee County (KS) Public Library in Cybrary City offers Second Life patrons access to local government information, as well as local history and genealogy resources, and the Australian Libraries building in Cybrary City offers visitors books to read, links to their library catalog, and local agricultural resources. The Parvenu Tower on Info Island offers a wealth of information to Second Life residents within its ten floors. Organized by subject ranging from government documents to the humanities, each floor provides resource guides, databases, Web sites, books, and other information relevant to its topic area.

Subject Guides

The Stanford University Science and Engineering Libraries provide links to their library Web sites, as well as Web link guides for stem cell research and biomedical engineering, in their Cybrary City branch, while the Nova Southeastern University (FL) maintains a virtual Law Library and Technology Center within Cybrary City II. They provide subject guides, links to legal resources such as UN and government documents, and links to the library catalog and Worldcat.

Podcasts

The Medical Library on Health Info Island provides medical podcasts and videos, PubMed searching, as well as audiobooks and library events.

Conference Space

The American Library Association has its Washington, D.C., office in Cybrary City, which has information about the organization, as well as a conference room. It also has purchased its own island, called the ALA Arts Island.

Book Talks

The Talis SciFi and Fantasy Portal Library on Info Island offers book reviews, author biographical information, and readable books, as well as book talks and other library events. The Jack & Elaine Whitehorn Memorial Library in Caledon Victoria City offers patrons short stories, novels and collections, and dramatic works, as well as special exhibits, book talks, and library programming events.

HOW ARE LIBRARIANS USING VIRTUAL WORLDS?

There are over 450 librarians who are residents in the Second Life world. They are participating both as Second Life members and as librarians working to build virtual libraries. They are volunteering, learning, teaching, exploring, networking, and creating within this immense social environment. And they are teaching others to do the same.

Second Life Library Volunteers

Over 100 librarians are volunteering a minimum of two hours per week at staff service points throughout the world of Second Life. They are providing reference help for newbies still getting their sea legs within the game, organizing library events, designing special exhibits, and hosting island-wide tours. They are cataloging virtual collections, offering training and library instruction, and building collections. Librarians are volunteering in-world for their real-life libraries, as well as representing that of the Second Life Library.

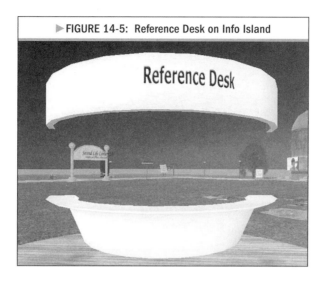

▷FIGURE 14-5: Reference Desk on Info Island

The Sights of Second Life

There are hundreds of amazing places within the world of Second Life—places to learn, relax, socialize, dance, gamble, or just watch the sun set. Here is a sample of some of the realm's more interesting places.

Svarga

http://slurl.com/secondlife/Svarga/8/123/22

Built atop a dormant volcano, the island paradise of Svarga was created for relaxation. Visitors can meander down ancient roads amidst lush tropical foliage and

▷FIGURE 14-6: Svarga

beautiful waterfalls, or enjoy the breathtaking views from raised footbridges. Residents may feed the birds, play musical instruments with friends, visit an oracle, or explore a castle. A guided tour of the island is available.

Caves of Lascaux
http://slurl.com/secondlife/Modesta/94/46/55

Based on the Paleolithic cave paintings found in Lascaux, France, these caves feature prehistoric paintings from all over the world. Visitors are led by candlelight along a tunnel leading into the main "gallery," where they can sit and enjoy the paintings or fly around for a better view. Although explorers must hike their way into the gallery, an exit teleport is provided.

Anime Island of Nakama
http://slurl.com/secondlife/Nakama/46/212/30

Fans of anime will love the island of Nakama created by Neil Nafus (aka Neil Protagonist), which is divided into four districts, each dedicated to a different genre of anime. The Kawaii Ku section is a tribute to the cute side of anime, such as that featured in the *Azumanga Daioh* series. The futuristic wasteland of Ayashii Ku, with its burnt-out buildings and barbed wire fences, is reminiscent of anime titles such as *Akira* and *Ghost in the Shell.* The Tonari Ku district is themed like the slice-of-life anime found in *Fruits Basket,* and the old-time Hokenjidai Ku neighborhood is designed like anime set in Feudal-era Japan, such as in *Ninja Scroll* and *Princess Mononoke.* The city can be toured by a train that passes through each district.

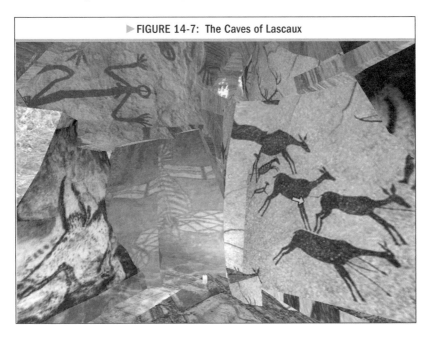

▶ FIGURE 14-7: The Caves of Lascaux

▷FIGURE 14-8: Nakama Island

Lost Gardens of Apollo

http://slurl.com/secondlife/Apollo/74/210/24

This ancient land of perpetual sunset is one of the most beautiful sights in all of Second Life. Take a guided tour on a magic carpet that takes visitors from the waterfall in Hyacinth Valley to the spectacular coastline views from the Apollo Towers and over the Bridge to Nowhere where residents lounge and relax. From the lush gardens to the secluded hideaways, this spot is a favorite pick for wedding receptions.

▷FIGURE 14-9: Lost Gardens of Apollo

▶FIGURE 14-10: Suffugium

Suffugium

http://slurl.com/secondlife/Suffugium/102/116/34

For a different type of shopping experience, spend some time in a futuristic cyber-punk dystopia called Suffugium, where police drones subject passing citizens to biological scans, and vending machines serve up Obey Cola. A hand scan upon entry will gain residents information about this refuge and its rules of conduct. Second Lifers are free to roam the streets, shop for goods, and read the conformist propaganda. Citizens are urged to report any suspicious activity.

MASSIVELY MULTIPLAYER ONLINE GAMES

There are many massively multiplayer online games available for would-be players who are seeking adventure, discovery, or complete immersion in another realm. Some are available for free, although most operate on a monthly subscription basis. MMOGs are persistent worlds that continue to exist and thrive even after individual players turn off their computers.

Second Life

www.secondlife.com

This innovative online universe is a second home to over 8 million "residents." Offering both free and paid membership options, Second Life allows players to choose their level of engagement. Although anything goes in this mature world, Second Life provides a separate Teen Second Life grid that is restricted to those between the ages of 13–17. Educators wishing to gain access must undergo a background investigation for security purposes.

Neopets

www.neopets.com

Aimed at 8–14 year olds, Neopets is a free virtual world that lets players create their own online pet and explore an interactive world. Offering over 160 games, auctions, shops, and spinning wheels of excitement and mediocrity, Neopets has attracted over 70 million pet owners to date. Neopets was purchased by MTV in 2005 for $160 million, and is partnering with Warner Bros. to develop a series of films based on the Neopets characters.

World of Warcraft (fees may apply)

www.worldofwarcraft.com

This subscription-based fantasy role-playing game boasts over 8 million players, making it one of the most popular MMOGs online today. Players can create characters, such as dwarves, elves, gnomes, and orcs, and lead them on adventures throughout this immense virtual world. Much like traditional RPGs (role-playing games), explorers are given a series of quests and are rewarded for experience and combat prowess, as well as magic skills. WOW players also can choose to adopt professions such as blacksmithing, first aid, and fishing.

Lineage II (fees may apply)

www.lineage2.com

With millions of loyal fans in both Korea and North America, this fantasy-based world continues in the tradition of its successful predecessor, Lineage. As with other MMOGs, Lineage II offers its players the opportunity to adopt multiple character races and classes for adventuring. Players may also tame and raise pets in the form of wolves, dragons, and other animals. Characters may join together in hunting parties or take part in siege warfare within this gaming system.

BEST PRACTICES

▶ **Form Partnerships**. Do not reinvent the wheel; the folks at the Second Life Library have laid the groundwork for libraries who want to establish a presence in Second Life. Libraries that are interested in building a virtual branch in-world should contact them about obtaining space on one of their nine Info Islands. Talk to other libraries that have set up shop in this virtual realm and ask them for advice about their experiences and feedback from their patrons.

▶ **Check Out Other Libraries**. Look around at other libraries in Second Life to see what types of services and programs they are offering. Think about which ones you would like to offer and what else you could bring to the community.

▶ **Be Prepared for a Learning Curve**. Making your way around this massive 3-D environment is a challenge for many players at the beginning. New players need to learn how to move their avatars around as well as to fly, teleport, speak to other residents, join groups, pick up and use items, buy and sell, and eventually build. In between, there are many nuances of this complex game to absorb. But there is plenty of help out there, including video tutorials, blogs, in-world classes, and of course, reference librarians. The best way to approach SL is to ease into it and call it a day when you start to feel flustered, and remember: it is new to everyone in the beginning. It is natural to be a bit overwhelmed at first.

▶ **Count on a Large Time Investment**. Second Life, like many other MMOGs, requires a significant investment of a player's time. In addition to learning how to "play" Second Life, there are many activities, experiences, and learning opportunities to occupy a resident's attention. If you are a library contemplating opening a virtual branch, you will want to consider the amount of time it will take to build that branch using SL tools, create in-world programs, and staff the library. Creating a library in SL is not just a matter of putting up a building and moving on— you will need to staff it with librarians in order to make it useful. Libraries will need to decide whether they have the resources to support such an undertaking.

▶ **Play**. Take advantage of the free account that is offered in order to spend some time in Second Life and test the waters. Explore the world, visit the Second Life Library, and interact with other residents. Discover if this is an environment that you want to become involved with, and if so, what can you offer that is not already provided?

REFERENCE

Gartenberg, Michael, and Jay Horwitz. "U.S. Massively Multiplayer Games Forecast, 2006-2011." Jupiter Research (May 11, 2006). Available (for purchase): www.jupiterresearch.com/bin/item.pl/research:concept/111/id=97277

►15

PRODUCTIVITY TOOLS

I n the spirit of collaboration proliferated by Web 2.0 comes a new breed of office applications to change the way we think about productivity. Eliminating the need to purchase and install costly software, Web sites such as Zoho Office and Google Docs & Spreadsheets offer access to powerful applications from any computer with a Web connection. These content collaboration tools enable virtual teams of document creators to liaise on projects, communities to cooperate on tasks, and individuals to increase efficiency.

Online office applications offer people the ability to author word-processing documents, spreadsheets, and slideshow presentations and to share them with invited collaborators. Some of these services even offer online database creation and project management software. These virtual office suites enjoy version control capabilities, which allow teammates to view the changes and edits made by others, as well as the ability to revert back to previous versions. Because documents reside online, they can be edited synchronously by everyone in a group rather than e-mailed back and forth.

Today, these free Web-based productivity tools are bridging the digital divide by providing valuable office applications to the masses. Web pioneer Google envisioned the benefits of such content creation tools when it acquired the Writely word processing Web site in early 2006. Spreadsheet functionality was quickly added to this offering. The Zoho suite of productivity applications has attained over 100,000 users since its launch in late 2005, and the Microsoft Office clone, ThinkFree, has over 250,000 registered members.

New online productivity tools are developed for the Web and render compatibility issues across platforms a thing of the past. They offer consumers access to applications as a service rather than a software purchase and provide seamless upgrades rather than downloadable patches.

PRODUCTIVITY FEATURES

Web-based office programs are offered by an increasing number of online competitors; however, the applications themselves share much of the same features and functionality. Some of these services present standalone offerings, such as 37 Signals' Writeboards, but most are moving toward integrated office suites with a single sign-on to all office applications. Google's Docs & Spreadsheets provides an illustration of the standard feature set available with these programs.

Toolbars resemble those found in traditional office programs, providing a familiar interface for working with documents. Through toolbar options, users can format fonts; insert formulas, images, and comments; and sort tables of data. While they do not provide the vast array of functions accessible through their desktop counterparts, these Web-based applications offer a low learning curve and portability.

Groups can **Collaborate** on a document by simply inviting teammates via an e-mail form. The author of the document may specify whether invitees can make changes to the document or have viewing rights only. All edits to a shared document detail the name of the person who made them, along with the date that they were made. Online office applications allow multiple users to work on a document at the same time.

Revisions made to a document can be viewed for its entire history. Documents can be reverted back to a previous stage in their development by simply clicking a revert button after choosing the desired version. Two versions of a document may be compared to one another in order to view the changes that were made.

File Options include the ability to export or save a document in another format. Users of online office programs are not limited to saving and storing their documents within these Web sites. They may create them on the Web and then save

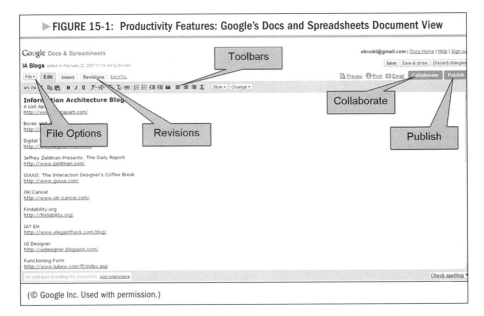

▶ FIGURE 15-1: Productivity Features: Google's Docs and Spreadsheets Document View

(© Google Inc. Used with permission.)

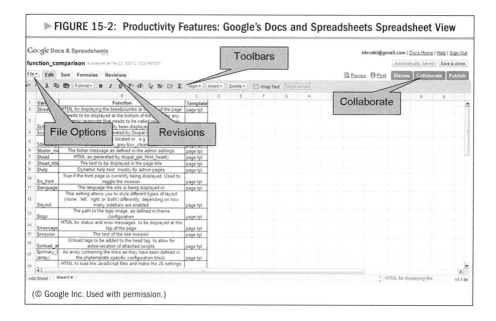

▷ FIGURE 15-2: Productivity Features: Google's Docs and Spreadsheets Spreadsheet View

(© Google Inc. Used with permission.)

them in various formats for offline use, such as .doc, .pdf, .xls, .csv, and .html. In addition to exporting documents to formats compatible with Microsoft Word, Excel, and others, these applications will also import a variety of file types.

Documents may be made public by publishing them to the Internet or by posting them to the author's blog. This is made easy by the **Publish** feature, which offers users this set of choices.

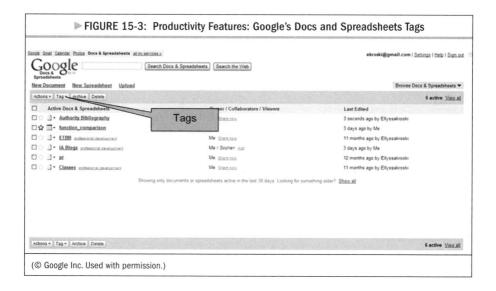

▷ FIGURE 15-3: Productivity Features: Google's Docs and Spreadsheets Tags

(© Google Inc. Used with permission.)

Tags are descriptors that may be attached to documents in order to organize them. Once these keywords are assigned to a user's files, they can browse them according to their own personalized categorization system.

PRODUCTIVITY TOOLS POTENTIAL IN LIBRARIES

An essential goal of libraries is to provide people with equal access to resources and tools for learning and productivity. Libraries strive to help close the gap between the technology haves and have-nots. New online programs that give people free access to powerful office applications represent another offering that libraries can add to their cadre of services. Additionally, these applications have the potential to be integrated into the library workflow, allowing efficient collaboration among staff.

Other Ways Libraries Can Use Productivity Tools

Offer Productivity Tools

Libraries have the opportunity to provide patrons with free access to productivity tools, offering them the use of online office applications they might not have access to elsewhere.

Collaboration

Librarians can utilize these productivity tools to collaborate on documents, spreadsheets, and presentations with other library staff, and can simplify long-distance collaboration efforts by sharing access to project files through these online applications.

Reduce Costs

Libraries have the ability to reduce budget costs by using free office software that does not require installation or server maintenance.

Upgrade Efficiently

Web-based productivity tools enjoy a continual state of improvement by developers who work to enhance their products based on user feedback. This eliminates the upgrade cycle, freeing libraries from the chore of monitoring and installing new releases and security patches.

PRODUCTIVITY TOOLS

Google Docs & Spreadsheets
http://docs.google.com
Google offers members the online word processor formerly known as Writely. Soon after purchasing the independent application in 2006, Google developed a

complementary spreadsheet application. All documents are accessible and presented in a central dashboard, which allows users to archive documents as well as mark them with stars.

Zoho
www.zoho.com

India-based startup Zoho offers people the largest collection of office applications and productivity tools on the Web today. In addition to the standard word processing, spreadsheet, and presentation software, Zoho also has a project management application and a database creator. They offer users the opportunity to create a notebook, planner, chat, and wiki. Their Zoho Virtual Office groupware product includes an e-mail client, calendar, task lists, and more. They have partnered with online storage applications box.net and Omnidrive, through which users can also access their services.

ThinkFree Office
www.thinkfree.com

ThinkFree offers a trio of productivity applications that are nearly identical to those found in the Microsoft Office suite. Members can create new documents, spreadsheets, and presentations within their own online office. ThinkFree allows its members to subdivide their creations into organizational folders, as well as offering the standard tagging feature.

Writeboard
www.writeboard.com

Less a word processor than an online text editor, 37 Signals' Writeboard was among the first on the Web to offer collaborative document creation. Writeboards are individual documents created by users through a simple interface offering version control and invitational sharing options.

SHARED CALENDARS

Web 2.0 calendars create an online space where people can plan events, invite others, and share their schedules with the world. These online calendars are available from any Web-enabled computer, and some via mobile devices. They offer versatility with personalized data that may be subscribed to and reused all over the Web. In addition, they provide an efficient way to organize and coordinate schedules.

An Airset Quicktake
www.airset.com

The Airset Calendar was created as an organization and planning tool for groups. Members of Airset can create and administer groups that maintain their own calendar, address book of contacts, task list, blog, and list of links.

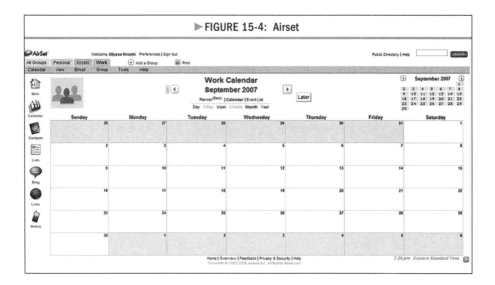

▶FIGURE 15-4: Airset

Each member of a group is assigned a role with various permissions regarding viewing, sharing, creating, and managing content. Airset has integrated Skype technology, enabling groups to make conference calls to other members with a click. RSS feeds are available for each group's calendar, blog, task, and link lists. Members can sync their Airset calendar into Microsoft Outlook or with their Palm device, and can receive event reminders via mobile phones.

Other Shared Calendars

Google

http://calendar.google.com

Google calendar users can not only schedule and share their calendars, but also invite others to upcoming events and track their RSVPs. Google calendars may be published to a Web page, accessed through a desktop widget, or via a mobile phone. Google start page users can choose to add a calendar module that will display their schedules within the personalized portal. Google Calendar can be used to share schedules among organizations with Google Apps.

30 Boxes

www.30boxes.com

A popular online calendar application run by only three people, 30 Boxes boasts over 80,000 registered members. They allow users to categorize their events by tag, and to color-code both tags and people. Members can create buddy lists and can share their calendars with others. 30 Boxes calendar widgets can be added to both Google and MyYahoo! start pages, and RSS feeds are available that can be subscribed to through Bloglines and other news readers. The company currently manages over 50,000 outgoing RSS feeds. Calendars may also be published to a blog or a MySpace page.

HOSTED STORAGE

Imagine a way to back up all of your files without having to burn them to a CD or store them in compartmentalized drives on your computer. New Web-based storage solutions offer just that functionality. Instead of e-mailing documents from work to home accounts for remote access, or carrying them on a Flash drive, members can simply upload them to a secure online folder. These convenient 2.0 applications offer the next wave in personal productivity.

An Xdrive Quicktake

www.xdrive.com

AOL's Xdrive provides 5 GB of free storage space to Web users who sign up for an account. Each person is given their own personal Xdrive space where they can upload and organize their files within folders, which they may share with invited collaborators.

Users can store their photo collections on their Xdrive and are able to create photo albums and slideshows. Music files can be backed up and arranged into playlists. Bookmarks can be imported, exported, and created on the fly. Those who already use AOL Instant Messenger may keep their AIM login information when they create their storage account.

▶ FIGURE 15-5: Xdrive

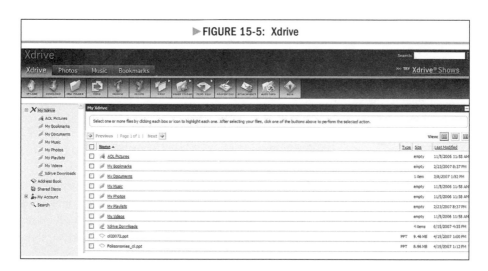

Other Hosted Storage

Box.net
www.box.net

Palo Alto–based startup Box.net enables members to upload, store, and share up to 1GB of information. Their 500,000 registered users can create friends lists that allow them to easily share and collaborate on documents through their network. Files can be organized into folders, tagged with keywords, and accessed through modules designed for start pages such as Netvibes, Goowy, Pageflakes, Live.com, and Google. A sharing widget is also available, which may be added to a MySpace profile or blog in order to share files with the community.

Omnidrive
www.omnidrive.com

Omnidrive provides the standard 1GB of storage space to its members who are able to publish their files to the Web or post to a blog. Their unique offering is their partnership with the online office application Zoho, which enables Omnidrive users to both create and edit Word and HTML documents from within their storage space. As with other hosted storage services, authors may share their files with invitees.

TO-DO LISTS

The age-old to-do list has been upgraded to an electronic version that allows sharing, organization, and anywhere access. New Web services offer the ability to create and manage multiple task lists that can be accessed in a variety of ways. While most of today's Web 2.0 start pages have added to-do list functionality, there are some standalone services that offer additional robust features.

A Remember the Milk Quicktake
www.rememberthemilk.com

Remember the Milk (RTM) enables its members to create to-do lists which are arranged and displayed in a tabbed interface. Users can include detailed information about tasks, set priorities for items, designate due dates, and tag tasks with keywords.

Listmakers may create contacts and groups with whom they may share their lists. RTM lists may be accessed via modules on Netvibes and Google start pages, and through Sidekicks and other mobile devices. Users can opt to be reminded about tasks with upcoming due dates by e-mail, IM, or text messages sent to their mobile phone.

▶FIGURE 15-6: Remember the Milk

Other To-Do Lists

Ta-Da Lists

www.tadalist.com

37 Signals' Ta-Da Lists offer an intuitive interface for people to create to-do lists quickly and easily. List authors can create multiple lists, subscribe to them via a list-specific RSS feed, and share them with e-mailed invitees.

BEST PRACTICES

▶ **Global Sign-In**. If you will be using productivity tools to collaborate within your department, you may want to consider setting up an account with a shared user name and password for your group, rather than sending out invitations to all of your colleagues for every document you want to share with them.

▶ **Set Deadlines**. Because documents can be edited at the same time by all members of a team, and collaborators are not rushing to send a document on to the next editor, it is important to provide a time frame for groups to provide their input. This is easily accomplished by requesting that all team members provide their edits and feedback by a specified deadline within your correspondence.

▶ **Offer Training**. If you want to collaborate with a group of people, such as a department or committee, be prepared to field questions and provide help to the less tech-savvy members of your team. Evaluate whether your team would be better served with a formal training session, more casual one-on-one drop-in sessions, or simply telephone or electronic support, and then make yourself available.

▶16

PODCASTING

tage two of the World Wide Web has brought with it an enchantment for amateur productions, opening the door for would-be talk-show hosts to become modern radio stars. Recent advancements in and awareness of Web 2.0 RSS technology, combined with the popularity of MP3 players, have given the ordinary person the ability to syndicate audio to the world. Through the art and science of podcasting, everyday people are gabbing their way to Internet celebrity by discussing everything from Harry Potter to the Catholic faith.

Similar to a radio or talk show, a podcast is a series of audio recordings or episodes that can be subscribed to via an RSS feed. People can subscribe to their favorite podcasts within a podcast aggregator, such as iTunes. As with a blog aggregator, such as Bloglines, a podcast aggregator—often called a podcatcher—will automatically update with the most recent episodes. Consisting of standard media files, podcast audio files can be listened to from a personal computer or any device capable of playing .mp3 or .mp4 files. Podcasts may contain image, video, or text files.

Declared the word of the year in 2005 by the *New Oxford American Dictionary*, podcasts are being used for language learning, interviews, tours, debates, course instruction, news, and current event coverage. Prestigious institutions such as Yale, Stanford, Princeton, and UC Berkeley are adding their class lectures and commencement recordings to the over 1.5 million podcast episodes available on the Web today. In the age of multitasking, these portable teaching tools provide not only the opportunity for people to rewind to sections they may not have understood, but also the ability to listen on the go.

Major media outlets, including ESPN, *National Geographic*, CNN, PBS, *The Wall Street Journal*, and NPR, are keen to the fact that advertisers are projected to spend over $400 million on podcasting by the year 2011—a number that will quintuple that spent in 2007 (Holahan, 2007). They have joined the podcasting masses and are using the medium as another form of distribution targeted at the 12 percent of U.S. Web users who have already downloaded them, as well as potential new users (Madden, 2006).

INSIDE PODCASTING

iTunes is the leading podcatcher on the Internet, its Top 100 Podcasts list accounting for 75 percent of all podcast traffic on the Web. Roughly half of those top podcasts are authored by mainstream media companies. Users can search, subscribe, and listen to podcasts within the iTunes application.

Education-related podcasts can be located within iTunes by navigating first to the Podcasting section of the iTunes store, and then selecting the category "Education." iTunes further subdivides the educational recordings into educational technology, higher education, K–12, language courses, and training categories.

Subscribe buttons are found with the description of each podcast, offering the listener an opportunity to receive new episodes automatically as they are published. Podcasts not found on iTunes can be manually subscribed to through the Advanced menu by entering the URL for the desired podcast feed.

Episodes of a podcast are listed in reverse chronological order, with the most recent episode at the top of the list. They include such details as name, creator information, description, runtime, price, and date of release. Most podcasts are free. Episodes may be listened to by double-clicking them, or downloaded by selecting "Get Episode."

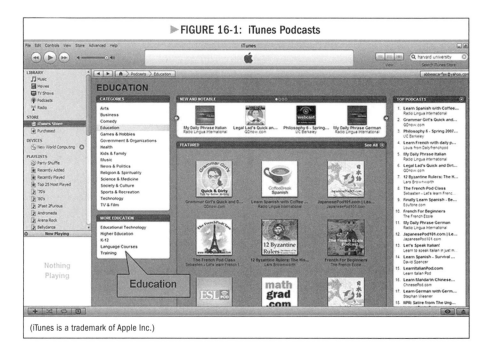

▶ **FIGURE 16-1: iTunes Podcasts**

(iTunes is a trademark of Apple Inc.)

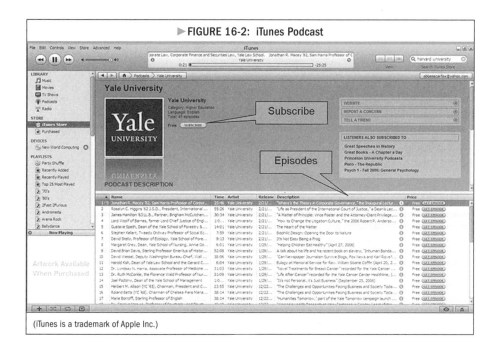

▶FIGURE 16-2: iTunes Podcast

(iTunes is a trademark of Apple Inc.)

HOW ARE LIBRARIES USING PODCASTING?

Libraries are using podcasting technology to communicate with and disseminate information to their patrons. They are creating podcasts to promote library programs and exhibits, instruct patrons how to better utilize library resources, present storytime readings, and provide book talks. Libraries are using this distribution platform to market their services, create oral histories, and archive lectures.

Sunnyvale Voices Podcast Series

www.librarypodcasts.org

In May 2006, the Sunnyvale (CA) Public Library began offering podcasts as an extension of their digital storytelling project. The Sunnyvale Voices project was a grant-funded endeavor that involved creating digital narratives made up of audio, video, and image files. These chronicles, as told by area residents, painted a picture of everyday life and work in early Sunnyvale, California. The Sunnyvale Voices stories were presented on VHS tapes that could be borrowed from the library.

Hoping to make these more accessible, Administrative Librarian Steve Sloan decided to offer the audio content of these oral histories to patrons as podcasts through a library blog. "Providing access to the stories through podcasting meant that people could access them anytime and anywhere from a computer rather than borrowing the physical item from the library shelves," Sloan commented.

▶ FIGURE 16-3: Sunnyvale Voices

Incidentally, the library has also made the full audio and video available on YouTube and Google Video.

Sloan utilized an audio recorder, the Edirol MP3 Recorder R-1, to create the audio posts, and chose to use a WordPress blog to distribute the podcasts because of its potential for customization. He implemented the Podpress plugin, which not only complements the WordPress blogging platform, but also simplifies the process of posting podcasts and offers an attractive display. The librarian chose to offer a single RSS feed for all of the library podcasts.

In order to publicize their 21 oral histories, the Sunnyvale Public Library issued a press release announcing the new Web site and published the podcasts in iTunes. Within ten months, they have received over 30,000 unique visitors to their podcasting blog and have been covered in a primetime news story about libraries using podcasting technology.

Sloan is satisfied with the technology choices made by the library and would use them again. He suggests that other libraries who are considering a podcasting program will want to focus on the content they might have to offer. "Don't podcast just to podcast," he advises. Sloan recommends that any organization creating podcasts also publish them in iTunes in order to reach a larger audience. "You want your content to be freely accessible right next to the latest U2 song. Place your content where your users are," he notes. (Steve Sloan, e-mail correspondence with author, March 2007)

Other Ways Libraries Are Using Podcasting

Oral Histories

The Pritzker Military Library (Chicago, IL) interviews recipients of the Congressional Medal of Honor, who share their stories of combat and courage, to create an oral history podcast series at: www.pritzkermilitarylibrary.org/podcasts

Library Tours

The Library@Mohawk College (ON, Canada) has created a BRAINcast series that includes tours of their library Web site, electronic resources, and library catalog, as well as a walking tour of the physical library at: http://braincast.libsyn.com. The Alden Library at Ohio University allows students to borrow an iPod to take a seven-floor tour of the library and gives them a choice to select the version recorded by a librarian or by a student at: http://tinyurl.com/2zwms6

Library News

The Georgia Perimeter College Decatur Campus Library has created a Listen Up! podcast series, which is a monthly library news and information update at: http://gpclibraryradio.blogspot.com

Book Discussions

The Muskingum College (OH) Library records discussions with book authors to produce their Author Talks podcast series at: http://mclibrarypodcast.blogspot.com, while the Orange County Library System in Orlando, Florida, hosts a teen booktalk podcast series at: www.ocls.info/podcast. The Curtin University Library in Western Australia produces a biweekly book review podcast at: http://library.curtin.edu.au/podcast

Library Events

The Moraine Valley Community College (IL) Learning Resoures Center records their library events and makes them available as podcast episodes at: http://tinyurl.com/37g2sk, and the Arizona State University Libraries present their patrons with a channel of podcasts featuring library news and announcements, as well as discussions of their library special exhibits, at: https://thelibrarychannel.blog.asu.edu.

Lectures

The Claude Moore Health Sciences Library and The University of Virginia School of Medicine Continuing Medical Education Program have archived their annual lecture series, "History of the Health Sciences," as podcasts at: http://tinyurl.com/39uapv, while the Paul L. Boley Law Library at the Lewis & Clark Law School in Portland, Oregon, offers make-up classes to students via its podcasts at:

http://lawlib.lclark.edu/podcast/index.php. The Western Kentucky University Libraries have created several podcast series, including "Faraway Places...with Strange Sounding Names," a lecture series that features talks with scholars who are researching in foreign countries, at: www.wku.edu/Library/podcast/ index.html

Storytime

The Denver Public Library in Denver, Colorado, hosts a "Stories for Kids" podcast series that presents storytime favorites in both English and Spanish at: http://podcast.denverlibrary.org

HOW ARE LIBRARIANS USING PODCASTING?

Librarians are creating, listening, and subscribing to podcasts on subjects as diverse as world history, motorcycling, and liberal politics. They also are taking advantage of the many learning opportunities these simple audio recordings provide. Organizations such as OPAL, SirsiDynix, and School Library Journal provide a wealth of professional development classes in the form of podcasts or .mp3 files through their Web sites.

SirsiDynix Institute's Web Seminars

www.sirsidynixinstitute.com

Librarians in the know listen to the free Web seminar podcasts from the SirsiDynix Institute. Featuring talks by well-known experts in the field, such as Stephen Abram,

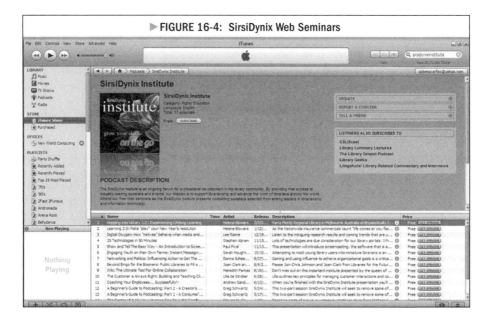

► FIGURE 16-4: SirsiDynix Web Seminars

Helene Blowers, Michael Stephens, Darlene Fichter, and Steven M. Cohen, the institute offers a valuable channel for professional development. Topics range from library branding and community building to developing employee and client relationship skills, as well as technology topics such as social bookmarking, screencasting, podcasting, and mashups. In addition to their Web site presence, the SirsiDynix Institute podcasts can be accessed and subscribed to through iTunes.

PODCAST RECORDING TOOLS

Audacity
http://audacity.sourceforge.net

Audacity is an open-source, free software program for recording and editing audio files. It is compatible with Windows, Mac, and GNU/Linux operating systems. Audacity offers multi-track mixing, built-in sound effects, copy and paste editing, and the ability to record as many as 16 channels at the same time.

Garage Band 3 (fees may apply)
www.apple.com/ilife/garageband

A part of the iLife software package for the Macintosh computer, Garage Band enables users to create professional-quality enhanced podcasts. With Garage Band, users can insert multiple tracks into their creations, including an artwork track and sound effects from the library of hundreds of podcasts sounds. Users also can create original music scores utilizing Garage Band's music loops and software instruments. Podcast interviews are conducted with ease utilizing the iChat conference capability, which records interviews with remote guests. Unlike simple audio recording software, Garage Band will publish podcasts directly to the Web and to iTunes upon completion.

PODCAST AGGREGATORS/"PODCATCHERS"

iTunes
www.apple.com/itunes/

Apple's iTunes is the largest podcatcher currently available. The term "podcast" was originally meant to be a cross between the terms "iPod" and "broadcast," and although that connotation is no longer relevant, it stands to reason that the creators of the popular MP3 player lead the aggregation pack. iTunes enables listeners to search for, listen, download, and subscribe to podcasts within its application.

Yahoo! Podcasts
http://podcasts.yahoo.com

The Yahoo! Podcast Web site allows much of the same functionality with regard to podcasts as does the iTunes application. Users can search, browse, download, listen, and subscribe to podcasts within their account. They are able to both rate and review content and, unlike iTunes, they can attach tags to podcasts. They present users with lists of the most popular and highest rated podcasts, similar to iTunes' Top 100.

Juice

http://juicereceiver.sourceforge.net

Formerly known as iPodder, Juice is a free, open-source podcast aggregator compatible across the Windows, GNU/Linux, and Mac platforms. A bit more advanced than some other podcast receivers, Juice is a downloadable program that manages podcast subscriptions. Downloaded over 2.5 million times, Juice has a directory of thousands of podcasts to choose from, is accessible to the visually impaired, and is available in 15 languages.

PODCAST SEARCH ENGINES

Podcast Alley

www.podcastalley.com

Podcast Alley indexes over 30,000 podcasts containing 1.5 million episodes. Users can browse podcasts in order of popularity within categories such as music, news & politics, business, technology, and religion & spirituality. Listeners who are interested in subscribing to podcasts are directed to the URL for the feed to be copied to their podcast aggregator. Users can listen to single episodes through the Web site, download episodes, and can comment on and cast their vote for their favorites.

Pluggd

www.pluggd.com

Pluggd offers an exceptional capability that searches for keywords inside podcasts. It presents users with a variety of ways to browse its directory of podcasts, including featuring editors' picks, by most popular, and by top rated. The collection of recordings also can be explored by navigating the tag cloud or clicking around by predetermined categories, including government & organizations, kids & family, comedy, and arts. Registered members can listen to, download, bookmark, and subscribe to podcasts within the Web site.

Podzinger

www.podzinger.com

Podzinger is a search engine that utilizes speech recognition technology to seek within audio and video content for keywords. Podzinger provides information about the exact time within the media file that a searched keyword appears. Users have the option to skip directly to that section of the podcast rather than having to listen to it in its entirety. Users can download and listen to episodes from the Web site, as well as access feed information for subscription purposes.

BEST PRACTICES

▶ **Establish a Mission**. You will want to establish a clear purpose for your podcast series before you decide to take on a project of this size. Although you will have the opportunity to explore different topics within episodes, there should be an underlying thread of continuity throughout.

▶ **Find a Hook**. Consider doing something unique, which identifies your podcast in each episode, such as an original jingle or sound effect at the opening, using the same announcement or announcer for each show, etc.

▶ **Listen to Popular Podcasts**. Take a cue from those that are successful in this medium by researching what works in the world of podcasting. Check out a wide range of podcasts in many different fields to find inspiration and pick up tips.

▶ **Consult Your Patrons**. Get ideas for subjects to explore by polling your community. Provide something valuable by asking patrons what they want and then filling that need.

▶ **Repurpose Existing Collections**. Think about the types of content your library might already have that could make an interesting podcast episode. Did your library conduct a series of interviews with local residents as a part of an oral history project? Has your library recorded author talks or lectures in the past? Turn these dusty archives into a new media offering.

▶ **Experiment**. You will not know what works until you explore and experiment a little. Try a few approaches at the beginning to see what sticks with your listeners, and be sure to ask for their feedback.

▶ **Allow Comments**. Put your podcasts up on your blog or other medium that enables user commenting. Allow your listeners not only to join the conversation, but to provide you with valuable feedback and insight into what works and what does not with your podcasts.

▶ **Publish Consistently**. You will want to set up a regular schedule to produce and publish your podcasts, such as weekly, biweekly, monthly, etc., so that patrons can count on when to expect a new show.

▶ **Provide Devices**. If your university library is offering audio tours, you may want to consider letting your patrons borrow an MP3 player for the duration of the tour. Although a good many students and patrons have MP3 players, there will always be some that do not. If you are providing a regular podcast show that can be accessed and listened to at a computer, you might want to let patrons borrow headsets in order to listen while they are at the library. Remember, the library may be the only access some of your patrons have to a computer!

(Cont'd.)

> **BEST PRACTICES** *(Continued)*
>
> ▶ **Market Your Podcast.** Whether you are creating a lecture series or a book discussion podcast, let the world know about your efforts. Issue a press release about your new show, spotlight it on your library Web site, and be sure to list your show with major podcast aggregators such as iTunes.

REFERENCES

Holahan, Catherine. "The Next Big Ad Medium: Podcasts." *Business Week* (February 14, 2007). Available: http://tinyurl.com/26p67q (accessed February 15, 2007).

Madden, Mary. "Podcast Downloading." *Pew Internet & American Life Project* (November 2006). Available: www.pewinternet.org/pdfs/PIP_Podcasting.pdf (accessed December 10, 2006).

►17

MASHUPS

One of the primary principles espoused by the new Web is the notion of developing technology and content in a manner that can be reused by others. This philosophy has led to the emergence of an innovative class of crossbred applications known as mashups. Taking bits of information and functionality from discrete sources to produce a unique application, these amalgamated creations leverage the imaginative efforts of the community. Technological free-for-alls, mashups are being invented by everyone from motivated power-users to corporate Web development teams.

A mashup is a hybrid Web application that combines two or more distinct sets of data and functionality from separate sources, blending them to form something new. The term is derived from the hip-hop music scene, where artists sample different music tracks to create a new and original song. Today's Web services are making this possible by sharing their technology through APIs (Application Programming Interfaces), most with generous licensing, and content producers sharing their data with RSS feeds. This open exchange enables Web users to discover new ways to use existing content while benefiting Web companies who learn from their experimentation.

Mashup makers are concocting mixes that present information as diverse as shopping matrices, maps of secret fishing holes, global skiing conditions, celebrity residences, and local cell phone reception. The Internet's guide to mashups, the Programmable Web, currently catalogs over 1,600 of these Frankensteinian creations, half of which utilize the Google Maps API. Currently there are nearly 400 Web-based companies that have issued public APIs, including such 2.0 heavyweights as Flickr, Technorati, Amazon, YouTube, Yahoo! Maps, and del.cio.us.

This book has explored many different types of technologies. As a final chapter, it is fitting to consider how they may be remixed to form a new generation of Web applications.

A MIX OF MASHUPS

Mashups range broadly in topic areas, although the majority of them tend to center around maps. Mashups can utilize any technology that has an API or RSS feed, which allows it to be shared. Mashup authors are not required to be—and indeed rarely are—affiliated with the producers of the content they remix. Here are just a few of the more popular mashups.

Flickr's Geotagging

www.flickr.com/map

Flickr's Geotagging feature is an incredible mashup between their popular photo-sharing service and Yahoo!'s mapping technology. Geotagging enables people to associate their photos with the place where they were taken by attaching location information to them. Photo-sharers can zoom into exact addresses on the map and drag-and-drop their photos onto it. The mashed-up map assigns exact latitude and longitude coordinates to images as metadata. Curious travelers and photo buffs can browse the map to view over 12 million geotagged photos.

HousingMaps

www.housingmaps.com

HousingMaps was the first acknowledged mashup and continues to prove one of the most useful of these tools. A combination of the real estate listings from Craigslist and the technology of Google Maps, HousingMaps presents a visual display of real estate listings for select cities in the U.S. and Canada. Covering over

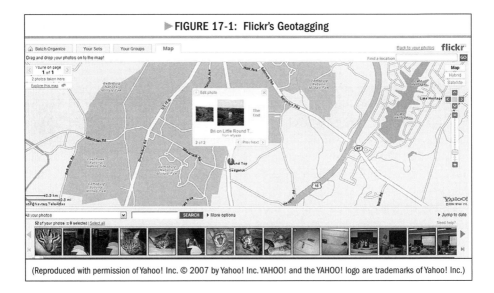

▶ FIGURE 17-1: Flickr's Geotagging

(Reproduced with permission of Yahoo! Inc. © 2007 by Yahoo! Inc. YAHOO! and the YAHOO! logo are trademarks of Yahoo! Inc.)

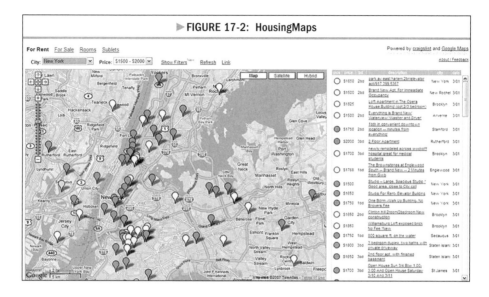

▶FIGURE 17-2: HousingMaps

30 cities, real estate listings can be browsed by properties for sale or rent, rooms or sublets. They can be sorted by price as well as by the number of bedrooms, date, location, and photo availability. Extra filters may be added to search listings by keyword, number of rooms, and whether pets are permitted.

▶FIGURE 17-3: PopURLs

PopURLs

http://popurls.com

PopURLs provides links to the latest news and multimedia from some of the Web's most popular destinations. On a single page, PopURLs displays the most recent headlines from news sites Digg, reddit, Newsvine, Metafilter, Tailrank, Google News, Yahoo! News, Netscape, Wired, Slashdot, Boing Boing, Fark, NowPublic, Shoutwire, and DZone. They present the latest bookmarks from del.icio.us, Furl, and Clipmarks, as well as the newest photos from Flickr and videos from YouTube, iFilm, Metacafe, Videosift, and AOL Video. PopURLs combines data from over 50 Web sites in one aesthetically organized page, making it an indispensable information resource.

ChicagoCrime.org

www.chicagocrime.org

Not affiliated with either Google Maps or the Chicago Police Department, ChicagoCrime.org combines data from the two entities into an illustrated representation of the city's crime locations. The application can be browsed by 75 different crime types, as well as by street, date, police district, zip code, or ward. Crimes also can be browsed by over 80 location types where the offenses occurred, such as a cemetery, abandoned building, taxicab, alley, or nursing home. Users of this application have the opportunity to draw a route on the map, such as a path normally walked, or a child's route to school, which will display all crimes that took place there.

▶ FIGURE 17-4: ChicagoCrime.org

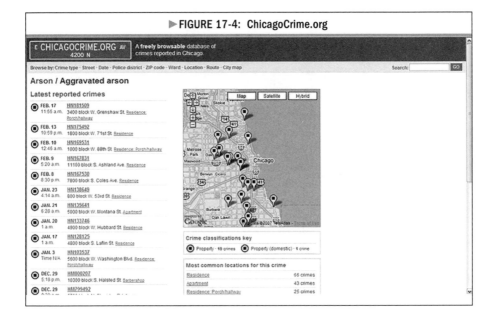

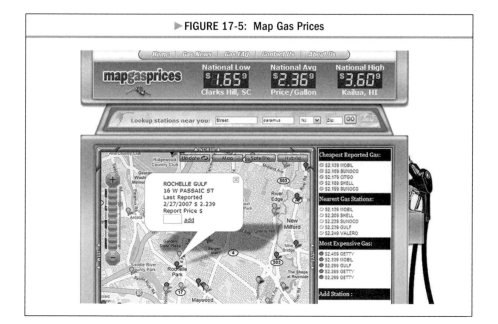

▶FIGURE 17-5: Map Gas Prices

Map Gas Prices

www.mapgasprices.com

The creators of the MapSexOffenders.com use the Google API to plot gas prices across the United States. Users can enter their location to compare prices among over 110,000 gas stations throughout the country. The cheapest, most expensive, and closest gas stations are presented along the right menu; however, users can click any colored balloon marker on the map to find station information and gas prices.

VIDEO MASHUPS

Mashups do not necessarily have to be applications. They can also combine multimedia files, such as music, video, and photos, to produce a mashup creation. Note: While "Fair Use" covers much of this activity, copyright is currently being debated when it comes to using multimedia files within mashups. Everyone should be well advised to examine current copyright standards carefully before reusing this type of content. Here are a few examples of popular video remixes.

Brokeback to the Future

This parody of the popular *Back the Future* films has been viewed over 4 million times on YouTube alone. Combining the music and video clips from *Brokeback Mountain* and the *Back the Future* series, Brokeback to the Future presents a touching tale of friendship between Doc and Marty.

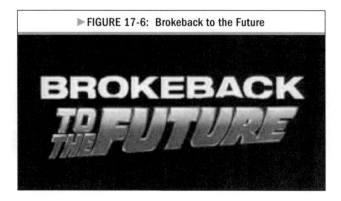

▶FIGURE 17-6: Brokeback to the Future

Scary Mary Poppins

A college student from Savannah, Georgia, remixed clips of the well-loved Disney film with spooky sound effects and the original score to produce a horror film trailer. A combination of deliberate and ominous scene takes with superb editing and effects, this re-cut is guaranteed to produce goosebumps.

▶FIGURE 17-7: Scary Mary Poppins

10 Things I Hate about Commandments

From the creators of "Must Love Jaws" comes this parody of the classic film *The Ten Commandments*. Re-cut as a teen romantic comedy starring Yul Brynner and Charleton Heston, this remix merges clips from the award-winning movie with music from major artists, as well as an original narrative track.

▶FIGURE 17-8: 10 Things I Hate about Commandments

HOW ARE LIBRARIES USING MASHUPS?

There are endless possibilities for mashups in libraries. Mashups can be created to display new library acquisitions on Web 2.0 start pages, combine searches of Amazon listings with library catalog searches, remix Amazon and other book reviews with the library catalog, add subject-specific Yahoo! Answers to library subject guides, and much much more. Libraries have already begun to experiment with the creation of these useful tools.

AADL Google Gadgets

http://tinyurl.com/34yj6b
http://tinyurl.com/2pz8ov
http://tinyurl.com/2toseb
http://tinyurl.com/2ulyac

The Ann Arbor (MI) District Library's Google Gadgets are a suite of widgets offering library patrons a customizable view of their library information. Four gadgets are available, which display the most popular items at the library, the newest items available, materials checked out by the patron, and items placed on hold. The gadgets can be personalized to present information about books, CDs, DVDs, or books on CD. These Google gadgets may be used within a member's personalized Google Start page or embedded within a Web site or blog.

These mini mashups between Google's gadget technology and the AADL's integrated library system were created by their systems administrator and lead developer, John Blyberg. Spurred on by the Talis "Mashing Up the Library" competition in August 2006, as well as his work on a similar project, Blyberg decided to undertake the challenge. "I've always thought that drawing data 'out' of traditional sources and making it available in a more ubiquitous form would make the library experience more natural and seamless to users," he said.

Blyberg decided to utilize the Google Gadget API to create his mashup due to its accessibility and powerful ability to parse remote XML. "Google Gadgets are actually an excellent catalyst for mashups. Their API is extensive and easy to use," he advised.

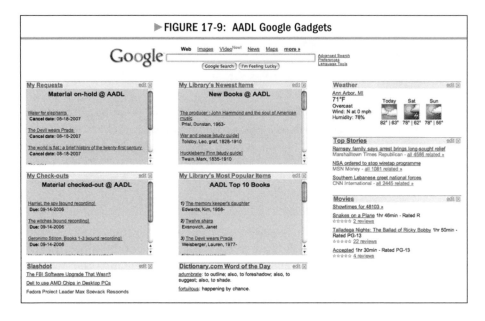
►FIGURE 17-9: AADL Google Gadgets

Blyberg and the library informed their patrons about the gadgets through word-of-mouth and blogging, and have already received positive feedback indicating patron adoption. Blyberg was quite satisfied with the Google technology and would recommend it to others considering a similar endeavor. "By putting that information on a portal page via a Google Gadget, that information passes in front of the patron's eye far more frequently and begins to build a sense of an 'omnipresent' library," he concluded. Blyberg claimed first prize in the Talis mashup contest with his Google Gadgets. (John Blyberg, e-mail correspondence with author, March 2007)

Other Ways Libraries Are Using Mashups

Amazon and the Library Catalog

Created using the Adobeflex technology, E41ST is a book lover's tool for browsing Amazon's virtual bookshelves and easily cross-checking interesting titles with a local library catalog at: www.amitgupta.info/E41ST, while the lead analyst for InfoWorld, Jon Udell, has created a Library Lookup bookmarklet, which enables users to look up books they discover on Amazon or Barnes & Noble in their local library catalog, at: http://tinyurl.com/4adt

Barnes & Noble and Catalog Searching

The Hennepin County (MN) Library offers its patrons a Barnes & Noble/HCL lookup tool, which allows them to check their library for availability of titles found on the Barnes & Noble Web site, at: http://tinyurl.com/29zxr4

Libraries and Google Book Search

Wayne State University (MI) has a Google Books Linky, which combines a library catalog search within the Google Book Search, at: http://userscripts.org/scripts/how/3415

Branch Location Maps

Libraries411.com is a mashup presenting more than 20,000 public library loca-
tions in the U.S. and Canada on a Google or Yahoo! map at: www.libraries411.com.
Similarly, Find a Library in Alberta, Canada, displays public libraries within the
Canadian province and links to their library Web sites at: http://tinyurl.com/yo9ab5

FINDING MASHUPS

Programmable Web

www.programmableweb.com

The Programmable Web is the go-to resource to discover Internet mashups. In-
dexing over 1,600 mashups and 400 APIs, the Web site provides a comprehensive
view of the mashup scene. Each mashup listing contains detailed information
about APIs used, author, tags, user rating, and related remixes.

MASHUP TOOLS

Yahoo! Pipes

http://pipes.yahoo.com

Yahoo! Pipes is a visual editor that lets users mix APIs, RSS, and other feed types to
create new mashups. Yahoo! provides starter "pipes" for users to edit. Users can
create pipes from scratch or clone a pipe that was created and shared by another
user. Yahoo! provides documentation on how to construct pipes, as well as tutorials and a community message board.

Google Mashup Editor

http://editor.googlemashups.com

The Google Mashup Editor is a developer interface for the creation, testing, and
publication of mashup applications. Application designers can build new projects
using technologies such as XML, JavaScript, HTML, and CSS within the Editor,
browse and manipulate source feeds in the Feed Browser, and test mashups from
within the Sandbox. When complete, mashups can be published with a click and
are hosted by Google.

Ning

www.ning.com

Ning is a social network creator that allows users to produce community Web site
environments like MySpace or Facebook. Network founders can select from a

menu of social application functionalities to add to their Web sites, such as: photo-sharing, videosharing, blogging, and discussion forums. Ning communities can be made public or kept private. There are currently over 30,000 Ning social networks.

Google Maps API
www.google.com/apis/maps
The Google Maps API enables Webmasters to use a Google Map on their own Web sites. Users can add and overlay information on the map to create a mashup. Free for non-commercial use, users need only to sign up for an API key. Google provides extensive documentation, code examples, and function tables.

Amazon Web Services
http://tinyurl.com/yw9oec
Amazon Web Services makes several APIs and tools available for developers who are interested in creating mashups. The Amazon E-Commerce Service provides the product data from international Amazon.com Web sites, including prices, user reviews, and images for free. This e-commerce data can be reused by mashup creators to form new applications.

BEST PRACTICES

▶ **Collaborate**. Many libraries have already taken the initiative and have begun creating Web mashups. Do not reinvent the wheel. Use the existing code to build upon what peer libraries have created and think about how you can offer improvements.

▶ **Make Sure It Is Legal**. Whether you are creating a video mashup or an aggregation of RSS feeds, you will want to pay close attention to the terms and conditions of use to ensure that you are permitted to reuse third-party data and functionality.

▶ **Start in Your Own Backyard**. Think about what RSS feeds or other materials your library produces which are particularly popular with your patrons and consider how you could remix them with other development APIs, such as Google Maps, etc. (Map-based mashups are probably the simplest and are often a starting point for new mashup creators.)

▶ **Use Mashup Tools**. Use the mashup tools that are becoming increasingly more available, such as Yahoo! Pipes or Google Mashup Editor, which provide a development interface for creating new and interesting applications.

AJAX (Asynchronous JavaScript and XML): A new type of Web 2.0 technology that enables information to be processed without reloading a Web page, making for a more robust user experience. An example of AJAX in action is the new drag-and-drop functionality found in many new Web applications, such as personal start pages, as well as tabbed interface elements that can switch between menus dynamically without refreshing the entire page.

API (Application Programming Interface): A programming interface through which users can access the functionality of a Web application. When issued, APIs are freely available for use by the community. In keeping with the spirit of sharing and syndication key to the new Web philosophy, many Web 2.0 programs have made their APIs publicly accessible. They also have found that it is advantageous to leverage the power of the developer community, allowing people to discover new and interesting uses for their products, which they may never have considered. A popular example of an API is the Google Maps API, which has been used to create hundreds of mashups.

Avatar: An animated figure or image that represents a player within a computer game or other online community. Through their avatar, players are able to interact with the world around them in computer games, including speaking to other characters or players within the game, touching or picking up items, and exploring.

Biblioblogosphere: Consists of the community of blogs relevant to the fields of library and information science.

Bittorrent: A peer-to-peer file-sharing technology that maximizes the bandwidth of the downloader who simultaneously serves as a source for the download. Files and information to be shared are formatted into torrent file types, which are distributed via a tracker. Peers connect to the tracker to download the file while at the same time seeding, or providing the portion of the file which they have already downloaded, to other downloaders. In this way, the Bittorrent technology differs from other file-download systems that tend to lag as user volume increases. In the case of Bittorrent file distribution, the more people who are downloading the file, the better the network effect and the faster the system functions, because downloaders are also offering file information for upload.

Blogosphere: The global online community of Web-based journals known as blogs.

Bookmarklet: Consists of a button that resides on the Web browser that can be clicked to create a Web site bookmark, which is stored online within applications like Google Reader or del.icio.us. The bookmarklet is a mini application that submits the page information, including the URL of the Web page the visitor is browsing at the time of the click, to its parent application.

CMS (Content Management System): A software application that facilitates the creation and organization of large collections of documents and other materials, such as multimedia items. A Web CMS enables users to collaborate and create content, assign user permissions and roles, manage workflow, create templates, and publish material to the Web. A CMS makes technical tasks easier by providing tools such as a WYSIWYG editor and automatic RSS feed creation. A Web content management system can be as simple as a blog or as complex as a Drupal installation.

Deep Tagging: A term referring to assigning tags "deep" within a file, to describe only a portion of it. Presently, it is used in conjunction with video clips that can be deep tagged using several video sharing Web sites. Instead of tagging an entire video file, deep tagging allows the user to place descriptive keywords throughout the file. Users can jump to tagged segments of the video, similar to chapters or scenes within a DVD. Deep tagging makes relevant segments of video clips easily findable. Examples of video sharing Web sites that allow deep tagging are Motionbox and JumpCut.

DIY (Do It Yourself): A self-service model that empowers users and frees them from having to rely on human intervention. Web 2.0 developers embrace this DIY ideology and strive to provide users with a low learning curve, intuitive design, and tools that enable non-technical users to become self-sufficient.

Drupal: A free, open-source Web content management system that can be used to create community Web sites, intranets, or virtual classrooms. The functionality of the Drupal system is controlled through modules that are selected and activated by administrators. Creators of Drupal Web sites can choose to add functionality such as blogging, forums, groups, comments, and taxonomies to their online community. Customizable themes are available, which will display a uniform color scheme and font style throughout the Web site. Examples of Web sites using a Drupal CMS are *The Onion*, The Ann Arbor District Library, and *The New York Observer*.

Folksonomy: A taxonomy created as a natural result of user-based tagging, a feature found on many Web 2.0 Web sites, such as Flickr and del.icio.us. A combination of the terms folks and taxonomy, the term was first coined by information architect Thomas VanderWal. As users tag their own and others' Web-based content, such as blog posts, photographs, and bookmarks, their keywords are pooled into a collective ontology. Since the process of tagging is inclusive by nature, a folksonomy is representative of the culture and language of that community.

Joomla: A freely available open-source content management system similar to Drupal. This powerful PHP-based software program enables Web site developers to create community-based Web sites capable of publishing user blogs, news items, photos, and RSS feeds. Although Joomla has many capabilities upon installation, there have been over 1,400 extensions such as calendars, shopping cart engines, and banner advertising systems created by its developer community. Examples of Web sites utilizing Joomla are Gnomedex.com and the South Carolina State Library.

Leaderboards: Lists that rank the most active or "top" contributors on participatory Web sites such as social news aggregators, as well as answers communities such as Yahoo! Answers.

Long Tail: The term describing the niche interests of today's consumers. The phrase derives its name from the long "tail" that forms when these peripheral trends, products, or topics are mapped out on a power law distribution chart. When combined together, long tail interests far outnumber the few popular ones, making the non-mainstream a viable alternative for opportunity. This statistical turn of phrase was first popularized by *Wired* magazine's Chris Anderson who authored a book of the same name. In it, he tells that the long tail accounts for between 25 percent to 40 percent of Amazon.com's sales, and that one-fifth of all Netflix rentals are from titles other than their top 3,000. The next-generation Web recognizes and embraces the long tail. Consequently, Web 2.0 applications are designed to serve not only the widespread, but also the fringe interests.

Machinima: A new art form that involves the creation of short films from within a video game. These films are usually made using the camera tools from within the games themselves. First-person shooters (FPS) or role-playing games (RPGs) are the most common settings for these works. Although the game "Quake" first popularized the genre, the most well-known machinima is a series created within the "Halo" game, called "Red vs. Blue: The Blood Gulch Chronicles." The successful fantasy MMORPG, "World of Warcraft" has inspired several machinima creations.

Mashups: Hybrid Web applications created by combining two or more distinct sets of data or functionality to form something new. Oftentimes, mashups are combinations of two or more existing Web applications, such as the most notable Housingmaps.com, which is a combination of Google Maps and the real estate listings from Craigslist. As more and more Web 2.0 companies make their functionality publicly available through APIs and RSS feeds, the already significant number of Web mashups will continue to increase.

Meme: A contagious idea, concept, or line of thought that is passed from person to person, evolving as it persists. Most recently, the term has been used to refer to an idea that catches hold and passes swiftly through the blogosphere or online community. Accordingly, there has emerged a subset of news Web sites, called memetrackers, which report on the conversations currently taking place on blogs and major media Web sites about a particular topic, event, article, or meme.

Millenials: More commonly known as Generation Y. They are the generation born between the late 1970s and the late 1990s. They also have been called the Internet Generation, the MySpace Generation, and Generation Next. They have grown up with the Internet and are known to be tech-savvy and computer literate.

MMOG (Massively Multiplayer Online Game): Any online game setting that consists of a shared, persistent environment supporting many players simultaneously. The shared universe of a MMOG is persistent, meaning it continues to exist even when the player is absent from the game. A related term is the MMORPG, which stands for a massively multiplayer online role-playing game, a subgenre of the MMOG that takes place in a fantasy setting. "Second Life" is an example of a MMOG, whereas "World of Warcraft" is a MMORPG.

News Readers: Enable people to read RSS feeds in human-readable format. People can subscribe to RSS feeds from Web sites, blogs, people, tags, news publications, etc., within their readers to receive the newest items from those sources. Once they have subscribed to these RSS feeds, the news aggregator continually displays updated headlines, synopses, comments, or full postings from each Web source. By subscribing to these sites, blogs, people, tags, etc., via an RSS Feed in a news reader, people can view the headlines or synopses of only the newest items from that source, as well as those that have been recently changed.

Podcasts: Episodic audio recordings that can be subscribed to via an RSS feed. The term originated as an amalgamation of the terms iPod and broadcast, although they can be played from a personal computer or any device capable of playing .mp3 or .mp4 files. Most often, podcasts are aggregated within a pod-catcher such as iTunes. Today's podcasts may contain images, video, or text files as well as audio.

Podcatcher: An application that aggregates podcasts, just as a news aggregator such as Bloglines aggregates news feeds. As with a blog aggregator, a podcatcher will automatically update podcast subscriptions with the most recent episodes.

Portal or Web Portal: A Web site that acts as a doorway to other pages or information available on the Internet that have been aggregated based on a particular subject or theme, and can sometimes be personalized. Personalized portals such as MyYahoo! enable users to create their own combination of information resources to be displayed on their portal page.

RIA (Rich Internet Application): An application that offers increased speed or efficiency within its user interface. These applications utilize an intermediary client engine that communicates between the Web browser and the application's server in order to reduce the time taken to process requests for information. RIAs are able to offer users the functionality of offline software applications through a Web browser. Examples of RIAs include those that utilize JavaScript, Flash, Apollo, and ActiveX technologies.

Tag Clouds: The visual representation of the most popular tags in use by a particular Web site community at any given time. More popular tags are displayed in bolder, larger fonts, giving the visitor an idea of what is favored at a glance. This display is an alternative form of navigation and a new way to browse around a Web site. Many Web 2.0 Web sites provide both a global tag cloud for the community as a whole and a personal tag cloud for individual users to both browse and glean insight into their own tagging behavior.

Tagging: The practice of assigning descriptive keywords to items such as bookmarks, images, articles, books, and videos. Adding tags to online media and other matter enables Web users to classify them for later personal retrieval or for findability by others. As tags are added by individuals, they are collectively pooled to contribute to the Web site folksonomy, forming an organic taxonomy for that community. Many of today's Web 2.0 applications allow users to subscribe to tags to keep updated as new items are assigned that descriptor.

VOIP (Voice Over the Internet Protocol): A new type of telephone service that enables voice communication over a broadband network. Voice signals are digitized and conveyed as digital packets over the Internet. This type of broadband telephony provides significant cost savings to the consumer.

Widgets: Also called gadgets. They are small applications that display structured digital content, often through an RSS feed. Widgets can display content ranging from blog feeds, Flickr photos, Google documents, events calendars, and to-do lists. Similarly, these gizmos are an effective way of displaying updates of sporting events, stock quotes, and news. These tools can be utilized both on the Web and on the desktop. They can display as well as aggregate content, and can be dropped into aggregators themselves. These versatile applications can be found on the new breed of Web 2.0 start pages, portals, and community Web sites.

Wisdom of Crowds: A theory based on the premise that the many will always be smarter than the one. The philosophy is anchored in the hypothesis that, although a few people will offer an incorrect answer to a question, the majority of people will offer the right one and outweigh the mistaken minority. This theory was put to the test weekly on the popular game show "Who Wants to Be a Millionaire" with their "Ask the Audience" lifeline that had a success rate of 91 percent (Surowiecki, 2004).

WYSIWYG (What You See Is What You Get): An interface, or editor program, commonly utilized for HTML authoring. WYSIWYG editors enable Web site designers to create Web pages without any knowledge of HTML code, as they work within what is usually likened to an MS Word–like interface, seeing only a preview of what the document will look like upon completion, rather than technical code.

Zeitgeist: From the German meaning "spirit of the time," it is used on the Web to denote what is currently popular. A Zeitgeist for a Web site community will convey what is in favor at a particular time. It is often a container for "Most Popular" and "Top" lists of items, as well as tag clouds.

REFERENCE

Surowiecki, James. 2004. *The Wisdom of Crowds: Why the Many Are Smarter Than the Few and How Collective Wisdom Shapes Business, Economies, Societies and Nations.* New York: Doubleday.

RESOURCES FOR WEB 2.0 DISCOVERY

RECOMMENDED BLOGS

TechCrunch
www.techcrunch.com

Micro Persuasion
www.micropersuasion.com

Dion Hinchcliffe's Web 2.0 Blog
http://web2.wsj2.com

Read/Write Web
www.readwriteweb.com

Emily Chang's eHub
www.emilychang.com/go/ehub

GigaOM
http://gigaom.com

The Bivings Report
www.bivingsreport.com

Tame the Web: Libraries and Technology
http://tametheweb.com

Library Stuff
www.librarystuff.net

Librarian in Black
http://librarianinblack.typepad.com

Stephen's Lighthouse
http://stephenslighthouse.sirsidynix.com

ALA TechSource
www.techsource.ala.org/blog

InfoTangle
http://infotangle.blogsome.com

RECOMMENDED BOOKS

37 Signals. 2006. *Getting Real.* Chicago: 37 Signals.

Anderson, Chris. 2006. *Long Tail: Why the Future of Business Is Selling Less of More.* New York: Hyperion.

Krug, Steve. *2006. Don't Make Me Think: A Common Sense Approach to Web Usability.* Berkeley, CA: New Riders Publishing.

Locke, Christopher, David Weinberger, Doc Searls, and Rick Levine. 2001. *The Cluetrain Manifesto: The End of Business as Usual.* New York: Basic Books.

Morville, Peter. 2005. *Ambient Findability.* Sebastopol, CA: O'Reilly Media.

Scoble, Robert, and Shel Israel. 2006. *Naked Conversations: How Blogs Are Changing the Way Businesses Talk with Customers.* Hoboken, NJ: John Wiley & Sons.

Schwartz, Barry. 2004. *The Paradox of Choice: Why More Is Less.* New York: Harper-Collins Publishers.

Surowiecki, James. 2004. *The Wisdom of Crowds: Why the Many Are Smarter Than the Few and How Collective Wisdom Shapes Business, Economies, Societies and Nations.* New York: Doubleday.

RECOMMENDED JOURNALS AND PUBLICATIONS

Wired Magazine
www.wired.com

Business 2.0
http://money.cnn.com/magazines/business2/

Business Week: Technology
www.businessweek.com/technology

Information Week
www.informationweek.com

Publish
www.publish.com

Online Magazine
www.infotoday.com/online

Computers in Libraries
www.infotoday.com/cilmag

RECOMMENDED WEB SITES

Pew Internet & American Life Project
www.pewinternet.org

Alexa Traffic Rankings
www.alexa.com

INDEX

Ellyssa Kroski is a Reference Librarian for Columbia University as well as an independent information consultant, national conference speaker, and adjunct faculty member for Long Island University's LIS program. She has been working with Information and Internet technologies for over ten years and specializes in Web 2.0 technology. Ellyssa holds an MLIS degree from Long Island University and authors the blog InfoTangle at: http://infotangle.blogsome.com